God Bless you!

David Ring

LITTLE PEOPLE, BIG CHOICES

Psalm 127:3-5

Little People, Big Choices

Your child can learn to make wise decisions

J. DAVID PURDY

Christian Publications

CAMP HILL, PENNSYLVANIA

Christian Publications
3825 Hartzdale Drive, Camp Hill, PA 17011

The mark of ✟ vibrant faith

ISBN: 0-87509-442-2
LOC Catalog Card Number: 90-86212
©1991 by Christian Publications
All rights reserved
Printed in the United States of America
91 92 93 94 95   5 4 3 2 1

DEDICATION

This book is dedicated to my mom and dad and to Nana Lucy who:
Teach by example
Live by the Word and
Love by the minute.

ACKNOWLEDGEMENTS

My special thanks to Jim Clevenger, Jackie Deems, Dianne Key, Lucy Lutz, Erica Miller, Ann Purdy, Dorothy Purdy, Chris Reese, Donald Schaeffer, Terry Truffin, Dana Johnsen and many others for their encouragement, help and support.

CONTENTS

JANUARY:

Resolutions
Concept words: *wisdom, eager,
discernment, encourage*

FEBRUARY:

David and Goliath
Concept words: *strength, courage,
omnipotent, confidence*

MARCH:

Wisdom vs. Foolishness
Concept words: *foolish, moral, truth, trust*

APRIL:

Jonah and the Big Fish
Concept words: *omniscient, omnipresent,
obey, vigilant*

MAY:

Daniel and the Lions' Den

Concept words: *endurance, worship, diligence, zealous*

JUNE:

Family Skit

Concept words: *arrogant, avarice, hospitable, patience*

JULY:

Secular or Spiritual

Concept words: *naive, deceit, conscience, ignorance*

AUGUST:

The Prodigal Son

Concept words: *humility, integrity, confess, sacrilegious*

SEPTEMBER:

Getting to Know You

Concept words: *affection, disciple, contribute, generosity*

OCTOBER:

Faith

Concept words: *sin, repentance, salvation, reverence*

NOVEMBER:

Emotions

Concept words: *anxiety, apathy, timid, content*

DECEMBER:

Saying No in the Face of Peer Pressure

Concept words: *reputation, alcoholism, nicotine, chameleon*

Introduction

As we prepare our children for productive lives in the real world, consider the correlation to the world of sports. The serious athlete is intent upon developing to his or her fullest potential. This entails a thorough knowledge of the game, rigorous training and good coaching. Children also need the knowledge, training and coaching that committed parents can provide.

All loving parents desire for their children to lead fruitful and abundant lives. And yet, how many of us succeed in the process of earnestly and consistently teaching, coaching and training our youngsters? The fact is: It is not our desires that will impact a young life; it is the diligent pursuit of our goals that will make a significant difference.

We are the lead-off runners in a very special

relay race. It is a race against time and unrelenting cultural opposition. It is our start and our initiative that can enhance a smooth transfer of our values in the all-important exchange zone. It is the parent-to-child exchange that can eternally impact the outcome of the race.

HOW TO EXCHANGE SMOOTHLY

Our children will best adopt our values and learn to make wise decisions if we are constantly teaching them those principles and values most likely to afford them happiness and spiritual sensitivity. Providing a living example, building healthy relationships and teaching the essence of wisdom are the most important elements. They are the thrust of this book.

As you read through and ponder the material, may God stir within you the insights and enthusiasm necessary for effective teaching and coaching.

1

Teaching by Example

Wisdom is a quality that must be learned, but can it be taught? Certainly! There are many ways that parents can play an influential role in the development of wisdom in their children. But first, what is wisdom?

Although knowledge and wisdom are terms that are often and mistakenly used interchangeably, closer study reveals a significant distinction between the two. Knowledge is familiarity with a particular subject area. Frequently it involves the accumulation of facts and information. Knowledge is often formally taught in a school setting and is necessarily acquired to accomplish educational and vocational objectives.

For example, working knowledge of an eight cylinder engine can be very useful and profitable. But properly driving a 3,000-pound vehicle down the highway takes more than mechanical inclination. A person might be mechanical when it comes to things under the hood, but if he or she is maniacal behind the wheel, that finely tuned engine—not to mention the person—is headed for trouble.

Wisdom is defined by *Random House Dictionary* as "the knowledge of what is good or right coupled with good judgment."

While parents are only partially and indirectly responsible for the accumulation of knowledge, they are primarily and directly responsible for the teaching of wisdom and discernment. The wisest man of all time, with the exception of Jesus Christ, was King Solomon. Solomon authored the Old Testament book of Proverbs in which he writes:

> Listen my sons, to a father's instruction;
>   pay attention and gain understanding.
> I give you sound learning,
>   so do not forsake my teaching.
> When I was a boy in my father's house,
>   still tender, and an only child of my mother,
> he taught me and said,
>   "Lay hold of my words with all your heart;
>   keep my commands and you will live.
> Get wisdom, get understanding;
>   do not forsake my words or swerve from
> them." (Proverbs 4:1–5)

These verses assume that parents have "instruction" and "sound teaching" to share with their children. This "good judgment" and "knowledge of right and wrong" as defined by the dictionary is to be passed on from generation to generation.

ABSOLUTE TRUTH IS CONTROVERSIAL

Of course, simply accepting a definitive set of "right" and "wrong" values is controversial in this day and age. Truth is seen as relative in many secular and even religious circles. Situational ethics, secular humanism, the new age movement and the world ideology purposes that there is nothing absolute. Life is seen as one large "gray" area without the intrusion of such concepts as right or wrong.

Truth, like beauty, is thought to be in the eye of the beholder. In effect, each person becomes his or her own god. No wonder so many children are confused and disillusioned when parents are so wavering in their own convictions.

Today's attitude of wavering is analogous to the story about frogs in a pan of warm water. As the intensity of the flame beneath the pan is gradually increased, the frogs will eventually boil to death, oblivious to the imminent danger. In the same way it is easy for us to become insensitive and complacent as traditional values erode beneath our feet. However, as a basis for teaching wisdom to children it is essential to identify a solid foundation. Jesus said, "Therefore everyone who hears these words of mine and puts them into practice is like a wise man who built his house on a rock" (Matthew 7:24).

The fact is that scriptural truth provides the necessary foundation—that rock—for building wise and discerning children. That is not to say children from nonchristian homes do not use discernment and good judgment. I know many kids from unchurched homes who behave more like Christians than some Christians.

A Christian environment is no guarantee of well-behaved children. However, from God's perspective and according to His Word, it is only through Christ and His teachings that we can have real fellowship with God (see John 15). Further, Christianity gives the depth and means—the Holy Spirit—to walk wisely in accordance with God's principles and in the center of His will. Therefore, the morally straight nonchristian who rejects the Lord has missed the essence of wisdom and the abundant life— personal fellowship with God.

CATCHING ON

Psychologist Dr. James Dobson has expressed that values are not necessarily taught to children; values are *caught* by children. Although we cannot disregard the need to consciously teach values or principles of wisdom, I can personally attest to the fact that children really do "catch on" to things.

One afternoon my wife, Ann, and our daughter, Carolyn, then a preschooler, were having lunch together. As Carolyn picked up her napkin and began to wipe her mouth, Ann noticed how strikingly similar Carolyn's mannerisms were to her own.

"You use a napkin just like I do, Carolyn," Ann said. "Do you watch me a lot at the table?"

"No," Carolyn responded, "mostly I watch Daddy."

"Oh, why is that?" Ann inquired.

"Because his ears wiggle when he eats!" Carolyn giggled.

I'd been sitting next to that little girl for four years and I had no idea I was so entertaining. Her awareness was amusing but it was also downright unnerving. Youngsters do study their parents. Although it may not be a conscious effort, they learn much about life and lifestyles from mom and dad. It may be something as simple as a parent's idiosyncrasy (dancing ears) or as profound as a marital relationship.

Sometimes, however, the lessons we expect them to be learning take an unusual twist. One Sunday evening after listening to a sermon on marriage and divorce, I asked my nine-year-old son, Ben, what he had learned from the message. Without hesitation he answered, "Stay single!"

Wisdom in our children is closely knit to the values and moral fiber of our own character. Our parental attitudes and lifestyle will clearly reflect our values in the minds of our children. In Scripture Paul declares to his friends, "Whatever you have learned or received or heard from me, or seen in me—put it into practice" (Philippians 4:9). In effect, Paul was saying, "Do what I say *and* do what I do." Naturally, it stands to reason that if you spend a significant period of time with a child, your values will become his or her values. Children often become what we are, not necessarily what we tell them to be.

I know in our home if my son is overly critical of his sisters it annoys me. However, before I take steps to straighten out his attitude I'd be wise to check my own attitude. It is quite possible that in recent days I had been overly critical of him or perhaps I had been impatient with my wife. If so, it may not be a case of the child "acting up." More than likely the child is "acting out" what he learned from me.

Someone once wrote:

> If a child lives with criticism he learns to condemn.
> If a child lives with hostility he learns to fight.
> If a child lives with ridicule he learns to be shy.
> If a child lives with shame he learns to feel guilty.
> If a child lives with tolerance he learns to be patient.
> If a child lives with encouragement he learns confidence.
> If a child lives with praise he learns to appreciate.
> If a child lives with fairness he learns justice.
> If a child lives with security he learns to have faith.
> If a child lives with approval he learns to like himself.
> If a child lives with acceptance and friendship he learns to find love in the world.

A SOBERING THOUGHT

The magnitude of such impact is difficult to measure, but the reality of these words is certain. Just as surely as God formed us in our mother's womb, we parents are a principle force in the formation of our children's character development. It is a sobering thought, but our children are learning from us every day. And I don't mind telling you that I've choked on that thought more than once. *From me? They're learning from me?*

Sometimes we are teaching and we don't even realize it. For instance, if we imply that it is wise to be physically fit but fail to take care of our own bodies, the hidden message to children might be this: Physical fitness is a good idea, but it is not really worth the effort.

What are we teaching by continuing to watch a television program after the actors have spouted off a long list of four-letter expletives? Although we may have preached about the evils of profanity, the message is this: Obscenity is harmful when it comes from the mouth, but acceptable when it enters the mind.

If we expect our children to attend Sunday school regularly, but we spend the morning in bed or at the local diner having breakfast during Sunday school, the message is this: Religion and things of a spiritual nature are worthwhile but they are basically juvenile and unimportant.

If we preach about the virtues of honesty and respecting the possessions of others, then stick our grubby hands into our children's halloween bags after they've gone to bed, what are we saying? Either that honesty is more important for children than for adults or double standards are acceptable in our family.

The fact is, we model for our children how to think, how to respond, how to behave and how to live. The impact and impressions we have on our children should never be underestimated.

A SAD EXAMPLE

A child who lives with an alcoholic parent is much more prone to have a drinking problem than a youngster from a more stable environment. You would think that a child growing up in the midst of that trauma and stress would be committed to a life of sobriety. But that is often not the case. Why? Because the subconscious messages through the formative years were deeply implanted in the child's mind. Every day that child was carefully taught how to think and how to behave:

- When you are angry—explode. Never talk things out.
- If there is a problem, always blame others.
- Cope with life by using alcohol.
- Drinking to excess is *normal.*

- Deny any responsibility for your actions.
- Always put yourself first.

It is interesting that some daughters of alcoholic fathers tend to marry alcoholics. Once again it is not logical to experience pain as a child and subsequently choose to reenter that world of pain via marriage. However, conditioning very often prevails over logic.

The young lady may be attracted to the first guy to give her affection. Even though a drinking problem is evident, it doesn't register with her because drinking is normal. Furthermore, *It doesn't get any better than this,* she thinks. *I'll take him.* A daughter often chooses her life partner based upon her father's image in much the same way the old cliche about sons looking for a girl "just like the girl that married dear old dad" is often true.

Scripture tells us that the sins of the father are visited upon the children to the third and fourth generation (Exodus 20:5). Is this because God is cruelly punishing a child for his or her father's mistakes? No, it is simply a matter of parental influence or inevitable consequences.

Fortunately the cycle can be broken. One adult having a warm and loving relationship with a child has a tremendous effect. In essence, this adult can teach the child an alternative lifestyle. It has been said that the difference between children who were abused and become child abusers and those who were abused and do not become abusive is the presence of one significant, loving adult in their lives.

WE ARE THE SOURCE

Our children look to us as a major source of wisdom. Although we can never be perfect examples for them, we need to be headed in the right direction. Teaching wisdom to children is effective only as we conscientiously "practice what we preach and preach what we practice."

Beneath our kitchen clock Ann and I have stenciled, "Walk wisely, making the most of your time" (Ephesians 5:15–16). It is a gentle reminder for both our children *and us*, their parents.

2

UNDERSTANDING MISUNDERSTANDING

Brothers, stop thinking like children. In regard to evil be infants, but in your thinking be adults. (1 Corinthians 14:20)

Many psychologists make use of a client's childhood recollections as a means to treat adult problems therapeutically. The therapist will often ask the client to think back in time to an early childhood memory and recall the theme, who was there and the feelings experienced at the time.

The following is an example of a childhood memory as revisited by a woman in her mid 20s.

WOMAN #1: "I remember being all alone in our dimly lit dining room on a beautiful summer day. All the children in the neighborhood were in my backyard having a wonderful time."

THERAPIST: "How were you feeling about being inside?"

WOMAN #1: "I felt like the Lone Ranger. And I felt how lucky those kids were to be outside playing while I was in this stuffy old house suffering with the measles!"

THERAPIST: "Could it be that you still feel that life is unfair?"

WOMAN #1: "Yes. It seems that everyone else always gets the good breaks in life and I'm always the odd one out."

In this situation the therapist used an early childhood recollection to identify the woman's thought pattern as an adult. You see, we often view life as an adult much like we saw it as a child. If our conception of life and our "fit" in the world are accurate and appropriate as a child, we are likely to make "fitting" adjustments as an adult.

However, often we carry misconceptions with us from very early childhood through to death. This incorrect perspective influences our lifestyle and may cause problems with interpersonal relationships, self-esteem, etc.

For instance, woman #1 believes that she is always getting a raw deal. She paddles upstream through life fighting the currents all alone in her worn-out canoe, while everyone else is leisurely enjoying the ride in their yachts—that's just how it appeared for woman #1 through her dining room window.

The therapist needs to lovingly confront this woman with the fact that this is incorrect thinking. It is not true that the wheel of misfortune always points in her direction as she now sees it. As she becomes sensitive to this issue, when these thoughts come into her mind, she can recognize them for what they are: wrong thinking. As she works this through, in time she will begin to feel happier about herself and life in general.

In a second example, a young woman dealing with feelings of insecurity recalls a vivid memory from her past.

> **WOMAN #2:** "I remember as a four-year-old I was in the operating room of a hospital awaiting urinary tract surgery. All these people in masks were looking down at me."
>
> **THERAPIST:** "How were you feeling at the time?"
>
> **WOMAN #2:** "I was feeling alone and very vulnerable. The lights were very bright, and in the background I heard laughter."
>
> **THERAPIST:** "It is difficult for you to be the center of attention in a large group, is it not?"
>
> **WOMAN #2:** "Oh yes. I avoid that like the plague."
>
> **THERAPIST:** "And when you hear laughter in a

group your first thought is that the spotlight is on you, that you are the brunt of their laughter."

WOMAN #2: "Exactly."

THERAPIST: "Could it be that the laughter in the operating room was not directed at you?"

WOMAN #2: "Yes, I suppose so."

THERAPIST: "Isn't it rather presumptuous on your part to assume otherwise? I believe you have been carrying this misconception for some 30 years now. Isn't it time you recognize it as such?"

While I am not necessarily endorsing any particular psychological discipline, there is a great deal of truth regarding the power and influence of youthful perspective. It is also true that many of life's problems can be attributed to wrong thinking.

As you may know, anorexia nervosa is self-imposed starvation. One of the most frustrating aspects in treating anorexics is that they do not clearly see themselves or their plight.

In his cassette series *To Be a Woman*, Dr. James Dobson shares his experience with the problem in an interview with Jackie Barrile, a representative with Anorexia Nervosa and Associated Disorders Organization. The following excerpt from Dr. Dobson's interview illustrates the reality of deceptive thinking in this disorder.

JACKIE: "I tell several of [my clients], 'If you can believe nothing else for a while'—because there is so much confusion when they themselves are trying to get better, they want to understand so bad—'believe this: you are wrong. What you're listening to, what's going on in your head is a lie. If you can, believe me for a little while when I tell you you'll get better. You are listening to a lie.' If they can [they should] start saying that in their minds when those anorexic thoughts start bombarding them again and again, 'This is a lie.' "

DR. DOBSON: "Have you ever had a patient look in the mirror and see skin and bones and perceive it as fat?"

JACKIE: "Yes."

DR. DOBSON: "Isn't that amazing?"

JACKIE: "That's amazing; then we go back to 'That's a lie. You're wrong.' " [1]

OTHER MISCONCEPTIONS

Encopretic children suffer with another set of problems. Encopresis is the soiling of pants. It is most often characterized by a boy who carries certain resentment toward his father.

I remember counseling with a sixth grade boy, David, and his family regarding this problem. I suggested that the boy and his dad take a little hunting trip and spend some quality time together. After they returned home the boy's mother was surprised to find the situation had worsened. When I counseled with David, he revealed his true feelings about the weekend.

"It wasn't that great," David said. "My dad, my uncle and my cousin, Jimmy, went along. He's 13. My dad was all the time telling Jim how great he was. Then he'd ask me why I couldn't do things as good as Jim could. It really hurt my feelings and made me mad."

Since David would not verbalize his true feelings to his dad, his anger was expressed in another way. David needed to learn how to *talk* about his feelings rather than express himself in such an unacceptable and inappropriate manner. David's dad, on the other hand, needed to become more sensitive and accepting of his son.

Personally, I deal with my own set of misconceptions. I enjoy having things rather neat and orderly. Subconsciously, I also expect it to be done for me. Living in a home with my wife and three relatively young children, it is not realistic for me to assume that our home will be the showplace of the Midwest. It is even less fair to expect that this setting out of *Better Homes and Gardens* will come to life without my cooperation. My wife, Ann, has been helping me with this misconception for the last several years.

CHILDREN BELIEVE ADULTS

Children have a strong tendency to believe adults. Therefore, any labels attached to children by parents will undoubtedly influence their thinking and activity. Negative comments directed at their spirit can virtually strip a youngster of self-worth and shame him or her into feelings of inferiority. Furthermore, negativism will actually perpetuate undesirable behavior. In essence, it is a matter of self-fulfilling prophecy.

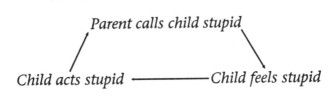

Many misconceptions in life are derived from believing untruths with which some thoughtless adult branded us years ago. I would encourage you to resist from using *any* personalized negative statements and strongly endorse positive "stroking" to lovingly build feelings of worth and dignity in your youngster.

The following list details some positive and negative messages that might be used in the same situations.

Positive Messages

"This is Mitchell, my good helper."

"This is Val, my sweet-spirited daughter."

"This is Teddy, my best little buddy."

"Now that I'm with you, all is right with the world."

"I like being with you, Emily."

"I really appreciate what a good listener you are."

"You bring such joy into my life, Tyler."

"I could never appreciate how much my mom loved me until I had you."

"I'm so glad God picked you to be in our family."

"There is something special about you, Paul."

Negative Messages

"Why can't you be like Jeremy?"

"You'll never amount to anything."

"Grow up."

"Big boys don't cry."

"You'll be the death of me yet."

"I'm sacrificing myself for you."

"You're bad (rotten, lazy, impossible, etc.)."

"You drive me nuts."

"This is Johnny, my little monster."

"I can't wait for school to start and get you guys out of my hair."

"I'm proud of you, just because you're my son."

"Life used to be so simple before you were born."

Our children are stockpiling memories every day. Hopefully they will be memories that reflect a positive approach to life, either because of our influence or in spite of it. However, there are certain misconceptions common to children that parents may be influential in redirecting.

GOALS OF MISBEHAVIOR

Don Dinkmeyer and Gary McKay in their book *Systematic Training for Effective Parenting* list four goals for misbehavior. Each "goal" is based on incorrect thinking.

The first goal is to be the *center of attention.* After all, each of us is born with the notion the universe revolves around us. Actually a baby does become the center of attention in most families. This is natural and to be expected. However, some folks never outgrow the need for center stage. In effect, they continue to believe the misconception, "I belong by convincing others they need to keep their eyes on me." Yet as Christians, where do our eyes need to be focused?

When Peter attempted to walk on the water,

he was doing just fine as he looked at Jesus. However, when he looked at himself and the perilous situation at hand, he began to sink. Part of growing up is understanding we cannot expect others to fall at our feet. Part of spiritual maturity is the recognition of Jesus as the One deserving of honor and glory. Anything else is merely a misconception.

A second goal involves the *quest for power or control*. By toddlerhood most children embrace the notion that family leadership is up for grabs. Although it seems incredible to think that is what is happening, it is true.

"In this corner, weighing in at 25 pounds, from Deluded Thinking, Illinois—Tommy Toddler."

"And in this corner, the tag-team, collectively weighing in at 315 pounds, from What In The World To Do, Arizona—Mom and Pop Parent!"

How presumptuous for a little one to believe he can take on this giant twosome! Yet here he is, a veritable Napoleon in diapers. And unless mom and pop set him straight, he will continue to push their buttons for years to come.

Several years ago I witnessed a scenario that epitomized this very issue. At mid-morning on the first day of school, a veteran kindergarten teacher came to my office utterly exhausted. In

25 years of teaching she had never encountered anyone like Mikey. After allowing her a few minutes to resume breathing she related the problem.

"Mikey is driving me crazy," she said. "He's ordering everyone around, including me!"

When she brought the little towheaded youngster in to see me, I posed a leading question. "How old is the boss in your room, Mikey?"

Without batting an eye he replied, "Five."

"How is it working out?" I countered.

"Not so hot," he admitted.

"Well, I'm not surprised, Mikey. Five-year-olds are not meant to be boss. A five-year-old's job is to be a good listener and a good worker," I explained.

Something known as "transference" was taking place. Mikey had been running his poor mother in circles tantamount to operating an electric train. "Now I'm going to run her around the tracks. Now I'll throw her in reverse. Now I'm going to derail her."

Of course, when he walked into the classroom the first day the faces and setting were changed, but the roles were typically the same. The classroom became the train depot, Mikey was still the freewheeling engineer and the unsuspecting kindergarten teacher became the little red caboose.

Scripture teaches that this type of thinking is not only incorrect, but unhealthy.

> Children, obey your parents in the Lord, for this is right. "Honor your father and mother"—which is the first commandment with a promise—"that it may go well with you and that you may enjoy long life on the earth." (Ephesians 6:1–3)

Nevertheless, some of us never do outgrow this power-hungry mentality. We feel we belong by always telling others what to do. The essence of secular humanism, a popular mindset of today, is autonomous power. It not only tells God He can't tell us what to do, it pronounces Him dead. Man is the creator and certainly not responsible to God. It sounds very much like Mikey and Tommy Toddler, doesn't it?

Conversely, the Bible states very clearly that God is the powerful One and worthy of praise. The God of Israel gives power and strength to His people.

> Praise be to God! *(Psalm 68:35b)*

> Every good and perfect gift is from above, coming down from the Father of the heavenly lights, who does not change like shifting shadows. *(James 1:17)*

For our Lord God Almighty reigns. *(Revelation 19:6b)*

Anything contrary is a misconception.

A third misconception involves *revenge.* It is the idea that we belong by hurting others as we have been hurt. This is a very natural reaction, but not necessarily a wise one.

I remember a neighbor years ago who took offense when we befriended another with whom he was "feuding." He refused to speak when spoken to and generally made known his disgust for our action. My initial reaction was one of *Hey, if that's the way you want it . . . so be it; who needs you anyhow? Don't tell me who I can be friends with. Who do you think you are anyway?* I didn't verbalize these thoughts, but I certainly felt them. Then we did a tough thing. We prayed for an "enemy."

After that we picked tomatoes from our garden and took them to his house. He was very surprised to see me and grumbled something about not needing any.

"Nonsense," I said, "we want you to have these." He was totally disarmed and the relationship was restored. Once again, this is a difficult lesson to learn because we practice incorrect thinking based upon our childhood understanding of life.

How about in our homes? The same principle of relationship still applies: "A gentle answer turns away wrath, but a harsh word stirs up anger" (Proverbs 15:1).

Anger begets anger and resentment. Though it is easy to react in anger to children because they have hurt, defied, annoyed or inconvenienced you in some way, it is the gentle response that will maintain or restore a relationship. "Do not be overcome by evil, but overcome evil with good" (Romans 12:21).

A fourth and common goal of children is to *convince parents not to expect anything from them.* In a sense the child "belongs" by keeping mother as busy as possible doing things for him or her that could really be done by him or herself. The more the child convinces mother and dad of his or her "helplessness" the more real it becomes to him or her.

At times, our daughter, Carolyn, would take great joy in having others "serve" her. (I guess most of us do!) Sometimes she would say, "Daddy, put my shoes on." To which I'd reply, "Oh honey, I don't think they will fit me!"

In her little way she has attempted to hook me into assuming her task. I have to be ever vigilant to remain "unhooked"!

Children feel capable only as they have been encouraged to assume responsibility for their behavior. If we deny them these opportunities, we are inadvertently reinforcing the notion that they are incapable. You've heard the expression "He thinks the world owes him a living." Where do you think he got such an idea? Perhaps as a child he should have been taught, "If a man will not work, he shall not eat" (2 Thessalonians 3:10). To think otherwise is a misconception.

The following is a list of misconceptions. Under each misconception are examples of parental responses that may either inadvertently reinforce the misconception or help to extinguish it.

MISCONCEPTION
- "I am not capable."
- "I need others to do things for me."
- "Others are positioned here in life to serve me."

PARENTAL RESPONSE THAT PERPETUATES WRONG THINKING: Parent overindulges the child and has minimal expectations.

PARENTAL RESPONSE THAT MAY ELIMINATE WRONG THINKING: Parent takes care of him or herself. He or she encourages and provides opportunities for the child to grow and succeed.

MISCONCEPTION
- "Nobody can tell me what to do."

• "I'm boss around here."

PERPETUATES WRONG THINKING: The parent continually fights or gives in to the child, is inconsistent and has poor self-esteem.

ELIMINATES WRONG THINKING: Parent demonstrates confidence, provides love with limits and maintains consistency.

MISCONCEPTION

• "Hurt others as others hurt you."
• "Other people are always out to get you."
• "Do unto others . . . but do it first."

PERPETUATES WRONG THINKING: The parent is angry, pessimistic, overly critical and overly sensitive.

ELIMINATES WRONG THINKING: The parent is a good neighbor, gives to and prays for others.

MISCONCEPTION

• "I never get all the love or things I deserve."
• Never satisfied, spongelike: "The more I get, the more I want."

PERPETUATES WRONG THINKING: The parent overindulges the child, models poor self-esteem and always provides immediate gratification.

ELIMINATES WRONG THINKING: The parent takes care of him or herself in a good way, doesn't pity the child and teaches the art of giving.

MISCONCEPTION

- "Nobody cares or understands me."
- Depressed or lonely.

PERPETUATES WRONG THINKING: The parent is too busy, gives minimal individual attention and either neglects or rejects the child's expression of feelings.

ELIMINATES WRONG THINKING: The parent nurtures, gives individual time to, encourages and actively listens to the child.

MISCONCEPTION

- Feels sorry for self—"Life is unfair."
- Martyrdom—"Others get all the good breaks."

PERPETUATES WRONG THINKING: The parent believes everything is "fate," complains about things but does nothing, exhibits bitterness and considers problems to be overwhelming obstacles.

ELIMINATES WRONG THINKING: The parent is positive, views problems as challenges to be conquered, believes in action and optimism rather than "fate."

MISCONCEPTION

- Bottle up your anxieties, put up a front—"If

you open up to others, you'll just get hurt."

PERPETUATES WRONG THINKING: The parent suppresses his or her feelings, denies feelings and always keeps feelings private.

ELIMINATES WRONG THINKING: The parent verbalizes his or her feelings, is genuine and open and minimizes "secrets."

MISCONCEPTION

- "I have to be perfect."
- "Win at all costs."

PERPETUATES WRONG THINKING: The parent is perfectionistic, has unrealistic expectations and stresses competition rather than cooperation.

ELIMINATES WRONG THINKING: The parent can relax and have fun, can acknowledge his or her mistakes and doesn't over-react to situations.

MISCONCEPTION

- "My happiness depends upon others."

PERPETUATES WRONG THINKING: The parent expects others to make him or her happy and always blames others for his or her own problems.

ELIMINATES WRONG THINKING: The parent takes ownership of both his or her happiness and problems and enables the child to entertain him or herself.

MISCONCEPTION
- "Do what others tell you to do at all times."
- "Listen to the voices outside your head."
- "I want others to make the decision for me."

PERPETUATES WRONG THINKING: The parent is authoritarian and makes all the decisions for the child.

ELIMINATES WRONG THINKING: The parent avoids power struggles, gives the child chores and allows consequences to take effect.

MISCONCEPTION
- "It's not my fault. He made me do it."
- "Why do you always blame me?"

PERPETUATES WRONG THINKING: The parent rationalizes everything, never admits to mistakes, doesn't follow through and continually engages in power struggles.

ELIMINATES WRONG THINKING: The parent doesn't "buy" into excuses, follows though unemotionally and is open about his or her own shortcomings.

Just as loving, earthly parents delight in the wisdom of their children, our heavenly Father rejoices when *our* lives bear the fruit of discern-

rejoices when *our* lives bear the fruit of discernment. Our goal in teaching children to be wise is not merely to keep them in line, but to enable them to enjoy the benefits of wise thinking.

God has given a promise to any adult or child wise enough to listen. "Thou wilt keep him in perfect peace, whose mind is stayed on thee: because he trusteth in thee" (Isaiah 26:3, KJV).

3

THE PARENT-CHILD RELATIONSHIP

Train up a child in the way he should go, and when he is old he will not turn from it. (Proverbs 22:6)

In order to be an effective teacher of anything, it is imperative that we have a willing learner. The old saying, "You can lead a horse to water, but you can't make it drink," is true. If the horse is genuinely thirsty and trusts the one leading it, the animal is much more likely to enjoy the refreshment. Likewise, when a parent and child have a warm and positive relationship, the child is much more likely to heed parental teaching.

If a relationship is unhealthy, a child may do things to spite his or her parents. For example, if good grades are important to parents, the antagonistic child may purposely do poorly in school.

Therefore, the degree to which children respond positively to your wise counsel will be directly related to the quality of your relationship. Consequently, as we pursue the task of teaching wisdom to children, we need to take stock of our relationships with them. For no matter how good our intentions or how bountiful the curriculum, the fact remains that children love learning only as they learn loving.

The other day my daughter Hannah expressed to me how much she loved me. I was quite touched, as you can imagine, and commented, "Thanks, honey! I wonder why you love me so much?"

"Because you loved me first, Dad," she responded.

First John 4:19 immediately came to mind: "We love because he first loved us." As Hannah pointed out, that's exactly how children perceive love and express love . . . in response to what they have received.

One of the best-known verses in the Bible is John 3:16. It begins, "For God so loved the world . . . ." What a wonderful truth! God, the creator and sustainer of the universe, loves you and me. His love for us is certainly essential, but the fact that He loves us is not sufficient. The reality of this truth was brought to life when God *expressed* His love—"that he *gave* his one and only Son." God's love was made personally relevant by giving His Son, Jesus Christ. In effect, God gave His love "legs." He activated His love in a meaningful way by moving into the midst of humanity and into the heart of mankind.

Children are not mind readers and we cannot expect our children to assume that we love them. Love needs to be demonstrated. And it is this continual expression of love that breathes life into a relationship. It is this love of life and a life of love that forms the basis for teaching wisdom to our children.

INFLUENCE VS. CONTROL

Strange as it may seem, parents really don't have a great deal of control over their children, especially as the children become of school age. Consider these situations. If my toddler decides to throw a tantrum in the middle of the department store . . . there it is! If my teenager decides to drink at a party or with his friends in the woods, can I really prohibit this behavior? If my 10-year-old decides to cut school some day, what can I do? I work six miles from her school.

Parents who are forever attempting to control their children are likely to become frustrated and unsuccessful in their attempts.

Furthermore, these efforts to control are very likely going to alienate the children they love so dearly.

It would be far more advantageous to focus our efforts and concerns on the one person in this world we really can control—ourselves. If I can control my responses to everyday situations effectively, then perhaps I can "influence" that youngster to demonstrate self-control in a department store, to make wise decisions about his or her lifestyle and to value a commitment to education.

The key word here is *influence*. We cannot fully control another person to think and behave in a specific manner. Nor do I think we would want to. Such tactics are more akin to brainwashing than child rearing. God doesn't brainwash you, does He? He has given us the liberty to make our own decisions. Of course, He has provided us with the means to make wise decisions. He encourages us in Scripture to pray continually, fellowship with other believers and meditate on His Word. But He has created us with a free will.

Genesis 1:27 reads, "So God created man in his image, in the image of God he created him; male and female he created them." This is what separates us from creatures in the animal kingdom. Animals behave instinctively. Birds, for example, are programmed by the Creator to build intricate nests typical of that species, even if they have never seen a nest before.

In like manner, male birds of certain species—even if taken from the mother bird and incubated and hatched in isolation—will perform a complex mating dance typical of that species. At the proper time and given the appropriate stimulus—his first look at Miss Lady Bird—he'll dance Michael Jackson off the stage. In fact, he will perform the exact steps and patterns other birds of his species have been doing for centuries.

Conversely, people learn best by experience and example. We need the opportunity to make decisions, rejoicing in triumphs and learning from mistakes. Forcibly controling another person—adult or child—will most likely set up an intense power struggle inviting anger, resistence and rebellion. Furthermore, it almost never produces the desired results.

FREE TO CHOOSE

In my book *Dads Are Special, Too,* I described a situation involving my youngest daughter, Carolyn, who was two and a half at that time. Although she had been toilet trained for several months, she began "irrigating" the carpet one afternoon.

Initially I reacted in anger, determined to stop this misbehavior through intimidation, lecture and punishment. Even though I managed to startle her at that moment, her wetting continued. It was only when I controled my response to the situation, matter of factly, in love, and provided an appropriate consequence that this behavior discontinued.

The difference? *She* decided that purposely wetting her pants was unwise and unprofitable. I *influenced* her thinking by lovingly confronting and using an appropriate consequence.

"Oh Carolyn," I said, "I see you decided to wet your pants instead of using the potty the way you used to do."

She looked at me silently. "Do you know what that makes me think?" I continued.

She shook her head no.

"It makes me think that you are not getting enough sleep," I said. "You see, little babies need lots of sleep, and little babies wet their pants, too."

She continued to look at me soberly.

"Honey," I went on, "when you wet your pants like a baby, I'll know you want to sleep like a baby and go back to bed. So the next time you want to go to bed, you just wet your pants and I'll know it's bedtime."[2]

She tested me twice. Each time I responded very calmly as I gently carried her up to bed. I kissed her good night and let her nap in her wet pants. In two days the wetting completely stopped. Where my forcible tactics proved unsuccessful, Carolyn made the decision to behave responsibly in relative freedom.

She was free to choose what *she* would do. I defused the power struggle by backing off. In a sense I was saying to her, "This is not my problem nor is it my decision. I'm glad *I'm* dry and get to stay up. Maybe you'll decide to stay dry, too. Good luck with your decision, honey. The nice thing about me is I'll love you whether you are wet or dry."

I removed all secondary gains she might have received from her antics, gains such as attention, power, revenge, etc. Ultimately there was no reason for her to continue. In her little mind she probably was thinking, *Nobody's paying much attention to me when I do this. They won't fight with me about it, and they don't even seem angry. For heaven's sake, who wants to stay in bed all day in wet pants!* In short, I controled *myself* using a loving, sensible response that resulted in Carolyn's wise and reasonable decision.

WISE ADVICE

The book of Proverbs, written by wise King Solomon and inspired by God, gives us some real insights regarding human nature. Consider the following verses and their implications for the parent-child relationship.

Proverbs 15:1 states: "A gentle answer turns away wrath, but a harsh word stirs up anger."
QUESTION: According to Scripture, what kind of parent produces a rebellious or angry child?
ANSWER: An angry parent. After all, if someone gets angry with us, one of our natural reactions is to get angry back!

Proverbs 15:4 states: "The tongue that brings healing is a tree of life, but a deceitful tongue crushes the spirit."
QUESTION: According to Scripture, what is the result of caustic and insensitive speech?
ANSWER: A broken spirit for the recipient. Some children don't get angry, but the self-esteem is damaged. They withdraw with hurt feelings.

Proverbs 18:14 states: "A man's spirit sustains him in sickness, but a crushed spirit who can bear?"
QUESTION: Which heals more slowly, a broken leg or a broken heart?
ANSWER: A broken heart. Most of us can remember some verbal "zinger" with which a thoughtless person labeled us years ago. The fact that it remains with us illustrates the lasting impact of a broken spirit.

Proverbs 16:32 states: "Better a patient man

than a warrior, a man who controls his temper than one who takes a city."

QUESTION: Which is more important: prestige, strength or self-control?

ANSWER: Self-control. Although our emotions are difficult to manage sometimes, anger directed toward children has basically negative results. Relationships don't flourish in the presence of anger.

MOUNTAINS OUT OF MOLEHILLS

Some of us by nature are nitpickers. We get so uptight about relatively meaningless issues that we really bug our kids. I once heard it described as rearranging the chairs on the deck of the Titanic as it plunged into the sea. There are plenty of people—including myself at times—who are entitled to the royalties of *Trivial Pursuit* because they were inclined to pursue trivial issues years before the game ever came on the market!

Charles Swindoll, in his book *Growing Strong in the Seasons of Life*, writes of Philip Melanchthon, Martin Luther's associate, who summed it up this way: "In essentials, unity; in non-essentials, liberty; in all things, charity."[3]

What things are really essential? In light of eternity what really matters?

Foster Cline, a nationally recognized child

psychiatrist, expressed three rules for a happy life.

> 1. Avoid power struggles. In other words, don't set up your child for a confrontation.
> 2. Pick your issues carefully. Is it an issue you can win? Is it really that important?
> 3. If it's a crucial issue, follow through and *win* it!

The next time before verbally accosting your child it might help the relationship to consider whether or not this is genuinely an essential or crucial issue. If not, it may be best to forget it.

Carolyn, our youngest daughter, was born barefooted and prefers to remain that way. From the day we first slipped shoes on her little feet, she insisted on taking them off. Would you personally consider wearing shoes to work as essential or nonessential? Unless you're a lifeguard or a karate instructor, shoes are essential. But how about a three-year-old going outside to play?

Many loving parents would cry *essential!* After all, the child might hurt her feet, get filthy dirty, and what would the neighbors think? Hey, whose feet are they? Who's getting dirty, and who cares what the neighbors think?

If she stubs her toe, *she* might decide shoes are a good idea. Besides, I'd rather Carolyn stub her toe than have her resent me for making her wear shoes. Her toes would be safe and warm, but our relationship might be cold and precarious. In short, wearing shoes in the yard is a nonessential. It is a power struggle not worth the hassle and an issue not that important.

PRESERVING PEACE

One of the reasons to grant liberty in nonessential areas is to preserve peace in the relationship. Another important reason involves the idea of thinking for yourself. If I continually remind Carolyn throughout childhood to remember her footwear, when do you suppose she will learn to become responsible for herself?

Lunch money is another good example. Children who continually forget their lunch money usually have loving parents who constantly bail them out. Mom or dad high-tails it up to the school with lunch money in hand. The child often comments, "My mom forgot to give it to me!" This is the same youngster who in adulthood will forever be foraging through the house in search of his or her lost wallet, grumbling at his or her spouse, "Where's my wallet? What did *you* do with my wallet?"

Why is it that in World War 2 there were

21-year-old fighter pilots flying combat missions and these days there are 21 year olds who can't find their socks? Well, parents, it doesn't have to be that way if we just give children the opportunity to think and acknowledge the good minds they've been blessed with.

A loving father did battle with his four-year-old over wearing inflatable water wings in the baby pool. Dad insisted she wear them although the water at the deepest point was only up to her waist and a lifeguard was close at hand.

The little girl protested she didn't need these "baby things" and the inevitable screaming match ensued. Dad eventually played his trump card. The ultimatum: "Either put those things on or we're going home!" They went home.

How sad. They had just arrived, and it was dad's day off, too. I admired dad's willingness to follow through as he did. Under other circumstances, hats off to dad. However, what really made this an unfortunate scenerio was the fact that this was unquestionably a nonessential issue. If a novice swimmer is confronted with five feet of water, the protection of water wings becomes a real necessity, but this little girl was making a good judgment that she could handle two feet of water in a supervised area. Dad demonstrated no confidence in his daughter's ability to think for herself. But what might happen, you say, if she stumbled in the water and came out sputtering and crying? *She* might decide water wings are a good idea!

Why is it so important that children, by adolescence, learn to think for themselves? Because if we, as loving parents, are always there to think *for* our children, we can't expect to witness discernment and good judgment *by* our children.

Of course, through our relationship during the formative years our values should be clearly modeled and carefully taught. Then as the children mature we can allow them the opportunities to form their own conclusions. The youngsters who most frequently get sucked into the cults, drugs and delinquent lifestyles either never learned a solid value system from their parents or their parents never learned to let go.

Below is a list of various situations. Which would you consider an essential issue? Mark those items E. Mark the nonessential items N. It would be a good idea and might prove to be quite interesting if you and your spouse did this separately and then compared notes.

___ 8-year-old watches R-rated movies.

___ 3-year-old refuses to comply with parental requests.

___ 6-year-old does not make bed exactly right.

___ 10-year-old wants to wear old jeans to school.

___ 9-year-old does not want to attend church.

___ 12-year-old wants to wear an earring in his ear.

___ 13-year-old wants to drink beer in the home.

___ 16-year-old wants to smoke cigarettes in the home.

___ 9-year-old gets Cs on her report card when she is capable of getting As.

___ 5-year-old does not want to eat her peas and carrots.

___ 7-year-old sasses his mother.

___ 8-year-old misses a spot while helping you wash the car.

___ 9-year-old puts down his sister, continually name-calling and insulting her.

___ 6-year-old dawdles in the morning and is almost late for school.

___ 2-year-old messes his pants.

___ 4-year-old doesn't want to wear shoes in the summer.

___ 10-year-old hasn't begun his science project, and it is due in two days.

___ 8-year-old is insisting on wearing eye liner and lipstick.

___ 11-year-old is listening to "hard rock" music in his room.

___ 9-year-old slouches at the dinner table.

___ 17-year-old decides to drop her college preparatory classes and decides a vocational school program is more desirable.

___ 5-year-old sucks her thumb.

___ 4-year-old wets the bed.

___ 6-year-old son would rather read than play ball.

___ 9-year-old insists on coming home for lunch rather than eat at school with his peers.

___ 6-year-old wants to sleep with a night light on.

___ 7-year-old wants to watch TV as soon as she gets home from school.

___ 5-year-old wants to sleep with you and your spouse.

___ 7-year-old wants to attend a sleep-over party at the home of a classmate whose parents are of questionable reputation.

___ 8-year-old wants to have a birthday party and invite all the boys in his class except one.

___ 4-year-old wants her hair cut short, but you think it looks better long.

Every parent either consciously or unconsciously selects the E or N many times during the course of a day. I can't tell you which of these you should consider essential. That is up to you to decide. But I will say that if the majority of your responses are E you could be setting yourself up for rebellion during adolescence. The reason: every situation presents a possible power struggle with the child. In like manner, every order or command invites a possible confrontation.

On the other hand, if none of your responses are E, I question the foundation of your child's value system. It might reflect the absence of parental involvement. Generally speaking, children who are out of control in elementary years come from homes where parents were not in control during the preschool years. Balance in this area is definitely an *ESSENTIAL*.

TUG-OF-WAR

It is not unusual for children to play the game of "getting" their parents. Many parents readily oblige by assuming a very "gettable" position. That is, they react to a given situation with amusing predictability. The youngster pushes the button and the parent reacts. Actually it is much like operating a remote control car, although running a parent is more exciting.

"Now I'm going to run her this way. Next, I'm going to run her that way. Now, watch her pop a wheelie!"

In effect, the child realizes—perhaps subconsciously—that certain childish behaviors set off expected parental responses.

One afternoon a mother shared with me her concerns regarding her six-year-old daughter, Heidi. The little girl was engaging in the annoying habit of pulling out her own hair. Obviously it was considerably more irritating to the mother than to the child.

At the rate this scenerio was progressing I wasn't sure which one would go bald first— mom was about to pull out her hair, too! Every time Heidi tugged at her long brown hair Mom blew up. Despite the fact that Heidi's hair was thinning, mom's predictable fireworks display made it all worthwhile.

As we talked I assured the mother that most eccentricities, although irritating to the parent, do not constitute a serious problem. We discussed the likelihood of stress, and I considered the possibility of a neurological disorder. However, this only appeared to be a bad habit that mom was inadvertantly reinforcing.

I suggested that mom give Heidi permission to pull every last hair from her head. "Heidi, I'll love you whether you have long flowing locks or no hair at all. Personally, I prefer hair, but bald might look good on you. However, since this behavior is rather personal, I prefer that you remove your hair in the privacy of your room. That way I don't have to see it or sweep it, and you can feel the warmth of

'Heidi-hair' comfort beneath your feet. Enjoy!"

When Heidi's mother responded in this way, Heidi went to her room for a few minutes, then returned to the living room declaring, "I don't want to pull my hair right now, Mom." And she didn't. In fact, it marked the end of hair pulling for both Heidi and her mother.

PROBLEM? WHO'S GOT THE PROBLEM?

The real "heart and soul" or "meat and potatoes" of child management is understanding the concept of problem ownership. It is really a simple idea to grasp intellectually, but often difficult for loving parents to carry through.

Don Dinkmeyer and Gary McKay, in their book *Systematic Training for Effective Parenting*, explain it this way: "To determine problem ownership, simply ask, whose problem is it? Once you determine who owns the problem, you are in a position to take action."[4] In other words, determine those issues, situations and problems that are essential and directly affect *you*. These issues need to be separated from those problems that affect your *child* directly. Why? For these basic reasons:

First, if you don't separate these problems out in the elementary years, it will precipitate rebelliousness in your teenager. Furthermore, understanding problem ownership will enable you to deal more effectively with your child and at the same time take care of your own needs. Finally, sorting out the problem will allow your child to become responsible and discerning.

If I ask you whose problem it is when little Johnny blows bubbles in his milk at the dinner table, what would you say? If you said, "Johnny's," I need to ask you another question. Does it bother Johnny when he blows bubbles in his milk? More than likely "liquid music" grates on the parents' nerves. So whose problem is it? Right, it's the parents' problem.

How about getting to school on time? Who does that affect directly? Well, you might say, "I'm the one responsible for Laurie, so I need to see that she arrives at school on time." Yes, but who has to walk into the classroom late? Who has to meet the teacher face-to-face? Upon whose record is her tardiness registered?

You see, getting to school on time directly affects Laurie. Even as a first grader Laurie should be setting *her* alarm clock, getting her things together and leaving the house on time.

Of course initially she will need some help in this transfer of duties. Both parent and child have become accustomed to things of this nature falling into the realm of mom and dad's responsibility. As an infant Laurie needed everything done for her. She was totally helpless, dependent, inconsiderate and out of control. Yet as a college student Laurie will need to be capable, independent, affiliative and in control. Therefore, somewhere between birth and adulthood a "changing of the guard" is necessary. It is up to the parents to facilitate this transition.

In this case mom needs to sit down with her some evening and say, "Laurie, for the longest time I've been making getting to school on time my problem. But you know, honey, I have confidence in you and I feel you can handle the morning routine without me. Oh, I'll be there to enjoy your company and to make breakfast for you. I'm also available if you have questions or need advice. Just ask me. I'm a virtual storehouse of wisdom. But I will no longer assume *your* responsibility nor will I mess up our relationship by nagging and reminding you. Our relationship is much too special for that!"

Mom might help Laurie plan for her mornings by making a checklist like this one:

MONDAY
__Library books __Lunch money __Make bed
__Brush teeth __Leave house by 8:45

TUESDAY
__Gym shoes __Lunch money __Make bed
__Brush teeth __Leave house by 8:45

WEDNESDAY
__Art project __Lunch money __Make bed
__Brush teeth __Leave house by 8:45

THURSDAY
__Gym shoes __Lunch money __Make bed
__Brush teeth __Leave house by 8:45

FRIDAY
__Show and tell __Lunch money __Make bed
__Brush teeth __Leave house by 8:45

Even if the child can't read, pictures of lunch money, gym shoes, books and toothbrushes can be charted. If mom can bite her tongue and really let go, it is almost certain that Laurie will become more responsible and the morning will be more enjoyable for both of them.

One day four-year-old Carolyn shared with her mom that she had lost her wallet. "Oh, Carolyn," Ann replied, "not again! When I was a little girl I would have loved a nice wallet like yours. You should take care of your things."

Moments later Ann heard Carolyn sigh and softly say, "I guess I never should have told you."

What an eye-opener for Ann. The little girl was saying that if you have a problem, mom might not be a good person to talk with. Personally, I consider Ann to be the best listener

I've ever known. However, she was not projecting this quality to her daughter regarding the wallet. Instead she became upset about Carolyn's problem.

Perhaps it would have worked out more agreeably if she would have empathized with Carolyn about how badly she must have felt losing her wallet. The consequence of not having a wallet until she saved for another would be sufficient to teach responsibility.

When Ben was nine years old, he broke his arm. The next day an orthopedic surgeon had to finish the break and set the arm in a rather painful procedure for Ben. A week later I saw Ben playing in the backyard and rolling on the ground with only the temporary cast. "Ben," I shouted, "What are you doing? Do you want that to heal? Do you want to have it set again? What's the matter with you?"

"I'm sorry, Dad," he responded with tears in his eyes. "I'll try to be more careful; but it is my arm."

I loved him so much I could not bear the thought of him reinjuring his arm. But he was right. It was his arm and his responsibility.

In retrospect I should have said, "It would be sad if your arm had to be reset, Ben. I hope you're giving all of this activity some real thought." How difficult it is for loving parents to let go.

I'm reminded of the familiar story about an episode that occured between a mother and her son on Sunday morning.

> **MOM:** Danny, it's time to wake up.
> **DANNY:** Z-Z-Z-Z-Z-Z-Z-Z.
> **MOM:** I mean it, Daniel. Wake up or you'll be late to church!
> **DANNY:** I don't want to go to church this morning, Mom. I'm too tired.
> **MOM:** But you have to go to church, Dan. . . . You're the preacher.

I can just imagine the door slamming and during the silence that follows, mom thinking, *Why can't he be more responsible?* Dan at the same time is grumbling, "When is that old lady going to get off my back?"

Well, as long as mom sweats the problem it's no sweat for the youngster. However, if mom doesn't sweat the morning routine, who will have to start sweating it? In this case it sounds as though mom has been sweating it out for a long time.

Dan never became the responsible young man mom has yearned for because she has enabled him to remain irresponsible. How? By never distinguishing between those situations for which she is directly responsible and those areas of responsibility which legitimately are Daniel's. She saw everything as *her* problem.

After all, Daniel was her little boy. Unfortunately, little Dan never grew up.

Here is a list of typical problem situations. Which of these directly affect the parent and which situations directly affect the child?

1. ___Chores not done.
2. ___Poor grades.
3. ___Loud music.
4. ___Forgetting lunch money.
5. ___Misbehavior in a restaurant.
6. ___Troubles with friends.
7. ___Getting to school on time.
8. ___Back talk, sassing, defiance.
9. ___Fear of school, the dark, etc.
10. ___Leaving toys in the living room.
11. ___Bedtime.

As I see it, numbers 1, 3, 5, 8 and 10 are problems that *directly* affect the parent. It bothers *me* when these things occur. Numbers 2, 4, 6, 7 and 9 are items that primarily affect the child. Although I am interested in these situations, my approach will be quite different from those that I consider to be my problem.

The bedtime routine is often a difficult one for both parent and child. While the amount of sleep directly affects the child, peace and quiet in the evening directly affect the parents. In a sense, what time the child goes to bed is the parents' problem; what time he or she goes to sleep is the child's problem. When you think about it, the parents can enforce the bedtime, but they are only kidding themselves by thinking they can make the child go to sleep.

NOT ALL ISSUES ARE PARENTS' PROBLEMS

Many loving parents see all of these issues as their problems. The reason for this may be the result of something psychologists refer to as a "blurring of egos." That is, the parent becomes emotionally entangled in the child's life. Of course most parents are emotionally involved in the lives of their children. However, in some cases the parent and the child virtually become *one* person in the eyes of the parent.

According to Dr. Burton L. White in his book *The First Three Years of Life*, a three-month-old baby begins to see him or herself as an individual, separate from his or her parents. Up to this point he or she mistakenly believes that those around him or her are merely extentions of his or her own person.[5]

For this reason a six-week-old infant is not ticklish, for it is impossible to tickle yourself. Consequently, as the baby perceives that the stimulus is initiated by someone other than him or herself, it takes on new meaning and new feeling.

It is the parent who may continue to struggle

with this concept of "separateness" long after it has become apparent to the child. This is a fairly common dilemma in parent-child relationships. Often there may be no discernable reason for it other than intense feelings of love. However, blurring of egos may occur due to marital conflict or parental insecurity.

The mother, for example, may "need" the child in an inappropriate way. In effect, the child may be filling mother's emotional vacuum because the husband is not. If the husband is cold, indifferent, critical or rejecting, mother may cling to the child for strength, warmth and purpose. The child becomes a surrogate spouse. This is not only unrealistic on mom's part but unfair to the child. The youngster is not designed nor emotionally equipped to meet mom's needs in this way. Furthermore, it is extremely difficult for a child to mature under this load of emotional baggage.

In a home where a child has suffered from severe trauma or illness it is very easy for parents to overstep their bounds of healthy involvement with the child. The tendency is to wrap arms around the child and smother him or her in love. The parents are so afraid of losing the child that they find it difficult to back off. Sometimes, however, they need to love the child enough to let him or her go. It takes real faith to believe that the child is capable in many situations while God is sufficient in every situation.

AN EXCEPTION

There is an exception to this rule of "direct affect" which needs to be addressed at this point. Issues that involve morality necessarily remain under the umbrella of parental responsibility, especially during the preadolescent years. For example, if my eight-year-old goes to a movie rated NC-17, it does not directly affect me, it directly affects my daughter. However, I am responsible for providing strong moral leadership, even if it results in a power struggle. This is an issue worth the hassle. I believe resistence will be minimal if you are tactful and begin when the children are very young.

Monitoring television, music and reading material during the formative years is an important part of shaping the child's moral growth and development. And moral development is not something about which we can afford to be totally objective.

God admonishes us,

> "But if anyone causes one of these little ones who believe in me to sin, it would be better for him to have a large millstone hung around his neck and to be drowned in the depths of

the sea." *(Matthew 18:6)*

We are obviously accountable for the moral and spiritual development of our children. Therefore, as we strive to promote responsibility in a child we must consciously preserve the innocence of the child.

In Corrie ten Boom's book *The Hiding Place*, she shares her father's response to her question regarding a rather heavy adult issue.

> He turned to look at me, as he always did when answering a question, but to my surprise he said nothing. At last he stood up, lifted his traveling case from the rack over our heads, and set it on the floor.
>
> "Will you carry it off the train, Corrie?" he said.
>
> "It's too heavy," I said.
>
> "Yes," he said. "And it would be a pretty poor father who would ask his little girl to carry such a load. It's the same way, Corrie, with knowledge. Some knowledge is too heavy for children. When you are older and stronger you can bear it. For now you must trust me to carry it for you."
>
> And I was satisfied. More than satisfied—wonderfully at peace. There were answers to this and all my hard questions—for now I was content to leave them in my father's keeping.[6]

Far too many children struggle with cumbersome adult suitcases, burdens that children are just not equipped to carry. The joy and innocence of youth should never be sacrificed in the name of responsibility.

Adult Suitcase Items	**Childhood Suitcase Items**
graphic violence	*what to do on the playground*
explicit sexuality	*age appropriate chores*
terrorism	*getting to school on time*
nuclear war	*deciding which baseball cards to trade*
marital conflict	*homework*
child support payments	*paper route*
bills	*music lessons*

Sometimes children need to talk openly about adult issues such as divorce. Communication in such cases is crucial. However, in concluding a counseling session of this nature I always ask the children to leave this issue in my keeping—in my suitcase. The youngsters are encouraged to return for more conversation but asked to leave this baggage with me and not carry it with them.

THE KID IS IN A JAM

Now let's look at ways to handle problems

that are really the child's problem.

What if little Jimmy comes home from school one day and says, "I don't want to go to school anymore!" Obviously the parent would be concerned about this revelation, but in perspective it is really the child who is directly affected. However, if mom assumes the problem is hers, she might react something like this:

"Oh no, Jimmy, what on earth happened? I knew something like this would happen up at that school. Honestly, I don't know what I'm going to do. There, there, tell me all about it, honey, and I'll make it all better."

When mother reacts this way it intensifies the problem in the eyes of the child, and at the same time, Jimmy does not feel understood. Furthermore, Jimmy is denied the opportunity to work through his problem.

It is interesting in many school phobia cases that when the parent handles the situation objectively and positively it stabilizes the child. Conversely, a hysterical parent invariably fosters a hysterical child.

An insensitive parent might cast off the child's remark by caustically saying, "First grade! You don't like first grade! Hey, wait 'til you get in junior high! It really gets bad then. You don't know how easy you've got it, boy!" Once again the parent denies the child the opportunity to feel understood.

Therefore, we do not want to overreact emotionally nor do we want to disregard our child's plea for help. The first step in helping a child work out his or her problem is acknowledging his or her *feelings*. In this case maybe Jimmy is experiencing fear. Mother might lovingly (but not overanxiously) respond, "It seems like you're afraid about something at school." Jimmy will let her know immediately if she is on the right track.

The parent needs to process the information in order to clarify for Jimmy what is really bothering him and what he can do about it. Consider the conversation at this point as a game of playing catch. Whoever is talking at the moment has possession of the ball. When I am finished talking, I toss the ball to Jimmy. He, in turn, keeps the ball until he has completed his thought, thereupon returning the ball to me.

A key issue in conversation of this nature is to keep the ball in Jimmy's hands as long as possible. In short, most parents talk too much. In fact, they're regular ball hogs! Jimmy really needs to talk this out with a good *listener*. The listener's task at this point is *not* to provide answers, but to give *feedback*. We simply reflect what we hear Jim saying by rewording his sentiments and perhaps tossing in a word or two that aptly describe his feelings.

> **JIMMY:** I don't want to go to school anymore.
> **MOM:** Sounds like you're really uptight about school.
> **JIMMY:** School stinks!
> **MOM:** I imagine school can be a real bummer at times.
> **JIMMY:** Yeah! I'd rather stay home with you, Mom.
> **MOM:** It appears to me that maybe you kind of miss me when you're at school, Jim.
> **JIMMY:** Well, sort of. I mean I never get to see you much anymore. You're either at some meeting or messing with Ricky or Julie.
> **MOM:** And you're feeling kind of left out.
> **JIMMY:** (sighs) Yeah.

By using the feedback method, Mom realizes that school is not the *real* issue. In fact, at this point perhaps *Jimmy* discovers school is not the real problem. It took a caring adult to help Jimmy process his thoughts and feelings and clarify for him what was really bothering him.

Once the source of the problem is clarified, Jimmy and his mom can begin to resolve the situation by exploring various alternatives. For example, mom might want to structure in some time to be alone with Jimmy on a daily basis for a while. Maybe Jimmy can stay up an extra 20 minutes in the evening or take a walk with mom after dinner.

Finally, mom can *encourage* Jimmy. "If anybody can handle school this morning, Jim, it's you! And I'm looking forward to our walk this evening. Good luck, honey—I know you can do it."

If necessary, mom can turn on the stove timer for 10 minutes each morning. During this time mom *listens* as Jim talks through his feelings. When the buzzer rings, the discussing ends and the encouragement begins.

GODLY COUNSEL NEEDED

Obviously, there are times when godly counsel is necessary and appropriate. One day Hannah came home from school and complained that a little girl had taken change from her lunch tray. She hadn't actually seen it occur, but some of Hannah's friends claimed they saw the whole thing. Later, on the playground, Hannah confronted the little girl who, in turn, denied it entirely.

Still miffed, Hannah was grumbling about the incident after dinner that evening, when suddenly her face went white and tears welled up in her eyes. As she had reached into her pocket her fingers had wrapped around the change from her lunch. Once again she recounted the unfortunate events of that situation. She had taken her friends' word and accused an innocent little girl of stealing.

Hannah was heartbroken.

After listening and empathizing, it was then appropriate to offer her some godly counsel. Hannah needed to apologize to her schoolmate. This was a difficult task to consider doing. Nevertheless, it is often the difficult and painful experiences that build character.

Hannah called the little girl and humbly apologized for the misunderstanding. Hannah quite naturally felt badly about wrongfully accusing another child. But while making that phone call was something she had not considered, it was necessary for resolving the problem. Not only was it encouraging to the other child, but it was only after the phone call that Hannah experienced a sense of peace. The burden was lifted and a lesson was learned.

An outline of our course of action would look like this:

1. Identify problem ownership. Who is directly affected?
2. Child's Problem
    A. Acknowledge the feelings.
    B. Listen and reflect. Good counsel provided when needed.
    C. Explore alternatives.
    D. Encourage.

Example: "Anna and Lynn won't play with

me." This is the child's problem.

> A. "Being left out really hurts, doesn't it?"
> B. Listen and reflect.
> C. "What are you going to do about it, and how can I help?"
> D. "If anyone can handle the tough situation, you're the one. I have confidence in you, honey."

THE PARENT IS IN A PICKLE

Now let's consider those situations you encounter that fall under the heading of "parent's problem." That is, the child's behavior is distressing to the parent. In such cases an effective parental approach involves four phases. Sometimes, when the relationship is especially good, the first step is all that is necessary. However, as Scripture relates in Proverbs 22:15a, "Folly is bound up in the heart of a child." Considering human nature as it is, most children will require that you effectively proceed through all four phases.

Just as the first step in helping children with their problems is *acknowledging their feelings*, likewise, the first step in resolving the parent's problem is *expressing* the parent's *feelings*. After all, *feeling* is one thing adults have in common with children.

Until the child becomes an adolescent, he or she does not have the abstract thinking capacity of an adult. For illustrative purposes let me use a humorous theoretical dialogue.

> **INTERVIEWER:** What do you think of Ronald Reagan?
>
> **EIGHT-YEAR-OLD:** I think Ronald Reagan was the greatest President we ever had.
>
> **INTERVIEWER:** What makes you think so?
>
> **EIGHT-YEAR-OLD:** 'Cause my daddy thinks Ronald Reagan is the greatest President we ever had.

> **INTERVIEWER:** What do you think of Ronald Reagan?
>
> **FIFTEEN-YEAR-OLD:** I think Ronald Reagan stinks!
>
> **INTERVIEWER:** What makes you think so?
>
> **FIFTEEN-YEAR-OLD:** Because my dad thinks Ronald Reagan was the greatest President we ever had.

Ah yes, the independent thinking of a teenager. Although teens can be downright cantankerous, they do possess the cognitive ability to think things through in adultlike fashion. They can comprehend the symbolic meaning of expressions such as, "people in glass houses shouldn't throw stones." A good thinking eight-year-old will interpret this as literally meaning to prohibit stone throwing as a means of protecting the glass. The good thinking adolescent can interpret the deeper meaning that involves treating others as you like to be treated or "if you can't take it, don't dish it out."

Therefore, it is best to relate with children in terms they can understand. Further, if I express my feelings to a child, I have given him or her the opportunity to be considerate of my feelings. For example, if I am on the telephone and my seven-year-old is banging on the piano, I can say, "Hannah, it's difficult to talk on the phone when you're playing the piano." Or I might say, "At the moment, honey, the piano music is making me nervous. I'd sure appreciate it if you'd wait until I'm off the phone to continue playing." One thing I need to avoid is setting my child up for a power struggle. It is difficult to rebel against an "I'd appreciate." It is relatively easy to rebel against an order or command.

The first step is simply stating how the child's behavior is affecting you. "Ben, it's difficult to see the game when you're standing in front of the television." I might add that this is equally effective when dealing with teenagers and other adults. Most parents will use such statements with other adults, but are usually not as consciously considerate with children.

Typically, a parent might respond, "Hey Ben, move it or lose it! How am I supposed to see the TV with your head in the way?" A strong-willed child would be tempted to stay right there or move just enough to comply but remain close enough to blot out part of the picture. A sensitive child would be hurt by the remarks and leave the room in tears. In any case, the child learns from his or her parent how to express feelings.

Consider the following verses.

> A word aptly spoken
> is like apples of gold in settings of silver.
> (Proverbs 25:11)

> A man finds joy in giving an apt reply—
> and how good is a timely word.
> (Proverbs 15:23)

Therefore, while we need to express our feelings to children, there is more to it than resolving an immediate dilemma. There is life and death in the power of the tongue. Hopefully, our words reflect wisdom and life; words that nurture are apples of gold.

GIVE THEM A CHOICE

Let's assume that step one was not effective in changing the youngster's behavior. The banging on the piano continues or the child remains planted in front of the television. Your next step is to give the child a choice.

"Hannah, do you want to play the piano soft-

ly or stop playing it altogether?"
"Ben, do you want to move away from the TV or move out of the room?"

In most instances the child will verbalize what *you* want them to do.

"I want to play softly."
"I'll move away from the TV."

The parent might respond with a wink and a smile, "Hey, now that's a good idea. What a wise decision."

Sometimes children develop whiny behavior and are no fun to be around. In this instance you can actually combine steps one and two by simply stating, "You know, honey, as much as I love you, I'm allergic to whiny behavior. And the way you're going I'm going to break out all over. You can either shut it off or leave the room until you get it together."

I can hear some of you saying to me, "Well, what does she care? She'll just go to her room and play games or do something else fun." Well, what do you want, a happy parent or an unhappy child? When you encounter a "parent problem," the goal is simply to make things better for yourself.

All I want is quiet when I'm on the phone or a good seat for the ball game. I hope my child is having the time of his or her life as long as

I'm having the time of my life. So go ahead and give the child a decision, the results of which will be pleasing to the parent.

FOLLOW THROUGH WITH CONSEQUENCES

The third step is simply to follow through with the consequences. "I see you've decided not to play the piano today" or "I see you've decided to go somewhere else to play. Adios."

Who decided what? Hannah, by her behavior, decided not to play the piano today. Ben, by his behavior, decided to leave the room and play somewhere else. The parent is not the villain and has done nothing to provoke the child to anger. It is important that the parent matter-of-factly follow through with the consequences that the child has behaviorally determined.

The task of determining appropriate consequences is one of the most important aspects of effective discipline. To help you in this regard there are four specific factors to consider when establishing suitable consequences.

1. CONSEQUENCES SHOULD ALWAYS RELATE TO THE MISBEHAVIOR.

There was a time when my girls would go into their bedroom and turn on their ceiling fan, which supports a four-bulb light fixture. Inevitably they would leave the room with the fan swirling and all the lights beaming.

Sharing my utility bills with them would make little impact. Coaxing, nagging and reminding them would get the job done, but only if I stood by and supervised the light switch. Therefore, we decided that anytime I walked by their room when the lights were on and they were not in, I would remove a bulb. I assured them that although the room might become progressively darker, I would replace the bulbs the following week for a fresh start.

After three days that first week the room was down to a solitary 40-watt bulb. Then an amazing thing happened. As their room grew darker, their little minds became enlightened. Now I could hear them say to one another as they ran down the stairs, "Did you turn the light off?" "No, didn't you?" Whoosh, up the stairs they'd go to save "watt" was left of their waning light fixture.

The following is a list of typical problem areas accompanied by some appropriate consequences.

Bedtime
• If I hear noise, I'll have to close the door. As long as I don't hear noise, the door will remain open.
• I'm available to read bedtime stories from 8:30 to 8:50. If you're in bed by 8:30 we'll have 20 minutes together. However, if you're

not in bed until 8:45, that five minutes will go by very quickly.

• For every minute you're late getting to bed tonight, your bedtime moves up two minutes tomorrow night. Good luck!

Mealtime

• If you don't eat dinner tonight, you can have it for breakfast tomorrow. We'll keep it for you in the refrigerator. Bon Appetit!

• If you don't eat your vegetables, you can forget about dessert. The next meal is breakfast.

• If you forget your lunch money, I'll help you out the first time. (Everybody makes mistakes.) After that, you're on your own. (Try not to make the same mistake twice.)

Chores

• If you pick up the toys you left in the living room you can use them tomorrow. If I pick up your toys you can use them next week.

• If you take care of feeding the dog, I'll take care of feeding you. You eat when the dog eats.

• Room cleanup is a Saturday *morning* activity. TV, phone calls, outdoor play and lunch are *afternoon* activities. How long do you want your morning to last?

Privileges

• If you work on your grades, I'll work on the car insurance. If your grade point falls below 3.0 (or whatever you determine) you pay.

• If you practice the piano, I pay for the lesson. If not, you pay for the lesson that week. (Keep a practice log notebook handy.)

2. THE CONSEQUENCE SHOULD BE SOMETHING THE PARENT CAN LIVE WITH.

Let's assume I received five courtside tickets for a Cavs-Bulls NBA basketball game. All week I'm "pumped up" to see Michael Jordan do his "air" show! Friday night rolls around and we're having dinner prior to heading for The Coliseum. Amid the excitement, however, I notice my daughter is not eating her beans. I suppose I could get tough and say something like, "If you don't eat your beans we're not going to the game!" Are you kidding? There's no way I want to miss that game. This consequence would be much more painful for me than for our picky eater. Furthermore, eating vegetables has nothing to do with going to a basketball game. I could say, however, "Whether or not you have popcorn tonight will depend upon what you do with your beans." After-dinner snacks relate to dinnertime eating habits. In addition, this consequence doesn't interfere with *my* needs, therefore I am more likely to follow through—which leads us to the next point.

3. BE CONSISTENT.

It has been said that the nature of the consequence is only as successful as the consistency with which it is applied. In other words, it's not just what you do; it's how you do it.

Foster Cline, a nationally reknowned child psychologist, makes the Las Vegas analogy. People are willing to play the slot machines numerous times with the hope that at some point *BINGO! JACKPOT!* In effect, it is worth staggering through four unsuccessful attempts when there is the possibility of a big payoff on the fifth try.

It's the same way in mom's kitchen.

> **BILLY:** Mom, can I have a cookie?
> **MOTHER:** No, honey, it's too close to dinner.
> **BILLY:** Please can I have a cookie?
> **MOTHER:** You heard me. No!
> **BILLY:** But I'm hungry. I'm starving to death.
> **MOTHER:** No, I said. We're having dinner in a few minutes.
> **BILLY:** It won't spoil my dinner. Please! Please!
> **MOTHER:** Oh, all right, have a cookie! Take three of 'em! Go on and spoil your dinner.

BINGO! JACKPOT!

4. CONSIDER YOUR ATTITUDE.

The benefits of a well-conceived consequence

are often diminished when administered by a frazzled, angry parent. Now I understand that it's difficult to retain your sanity when you are spending the day in "Munchkin Land." However, consequences are designed to teach, and no learning takes place when emotions get in the way. Therefore, matter-of-factly following through with a consequence is just as important as the consequence itself.

THE CHILD'S ATTITUDE

The fourth step in the disciplinary process is determined by the child's attitude. Let's look at our loud piano player situation again. As the consequence is carried through in step three, many children will compliantly walk away from the piano. Others are inclined to grumble a bit, but generally comply. There are times, however, when a child will defy your authority.

> "No!"
> "I'm not going anywhere. If anybody's leaving this room, it's you, MOM!"
> "Make me!"
> "You're not my boss!"

More passively resistant children may just choose to ignore your consequential statement. In such cases you might say, "Do you want to go with or without a swat?" However, if the overtly defiant child directly confronts you, a spanking is necessary. The manner in which this spanking is applied is crucial to its effectiveness. For example, spanking in anger has no real therapeutic value. Spankings are most effective when the parent is under control.

At the moment of back talk, defiance or disrespect, the child should be taken to a private place. If you're in a restaurant, take him or her outside or into the restroom. If you're at home, take him or her away from siblings, guests or other onlookers. You simply state the fact that your relationship is too special to tolerate his or her disrespect.

> The Lord disciplines those he loves,
>   as a father the son he delights in.
>   (Proverbs 3:12)

The spanking should be squarely dealt on the child's bottom. If the child has layers of diapers and clothes, your swat will probably have little impact. One swift swat on the bare bottom or lightly covered bottom is probably sufficient. Then hold the child in your arms and reaffirm your love for him or her. Some parents question the thought of saying "I love you" after a spanking. Isn't this confusing? It might be if that's the only time you hold your child and communicate your love for him or her. However, remember it is the behavior you are rejecting, not the child. To walk away from the child after a spanking infers the rejection of the child him or herself, rather than his or her misbehavior.

Further, the thoroughly confused child is the one who gets away with defiant behavior. The youngster who tests the limits and finds none, finds him or herself in a very precarious position—four years old and essentially his or her own boss. The child in this dilemma is generally insecure, anxious and unhappy. Ironically, so is the parent!

This issue of corporal punishment is highly controversial in some circles. In the case of a child caught with his or her hands in the cookie jar, after being told it was off limits, many authorities would simply advocate removing the cookie jar to an inaccessible location. But this is in no discernible way teaching the youngster self-control; it is merely removing the temptation.

In the real world temptations are not removed from us. We are expected to be responsible enough to resist and honorable enough to be trusted. If you are working in a clothing store, would you expect the owner to take everything in your size off the rack in order to keep you from walking off with the merchandise? Of course not. The employer expects self-control and integrity from his or her employees. However, if the cookie jars were always relocated during childhood, how would we learn to say no to temptation?

Those who so vehemently oppose spanking as an appropriate form of discipline in cases of defiant or disrespectful behavior have alternative forms of discipline. Sending your child to a "time-out" location may be sufficient. But let's say you send little Alicia to her room and she refuses to go. What do you do—carry her to her room? And if you tell her to stay in her room and she disobeys, do you carry Alicia back in? Do you lock her in the room? Or if you send Billy to his time-out chair and he jumps off the seat, do you tie him up or strap him in?

Where is the lesson in self-control when the child is banging on a locked door? How does the child learn to submit to authority while being harnessed to a chair?

The fact of the matter is, to be happy in life we need to behave responsibly. Many of the "bumps" in life come as a result of our inability to act responsibly in a given situation. Learning to accept authority is the very cornerstone of self-control and a prerequisite to spiritual growth. A child who belittles parental authority will have no respect for his or her heavenly Father.

The extent to which disciplinary action is effective is often contingent upon two factors—how strong-willed the child is and the consistency of the parent. Strong-willed children can be exasperating. Yet sometimes when they are hardest to love, we need to love them the hardest.

In summary, for defiant behavior an effectively applied spanking may be required. However, an effective spanking is not a lickin', whippin' or a "smack upside the head." Just hauling off and whacking a child is not only demeaning but can be considered abusive as well.

Effective use of corporal punishment considers the following factors:

RATIONALE: Did the child obviously and willfully defy you? Accidents, irresponsibility and forgetfulness do *not* warrant a spanking. Spankings are appropriate only as a child possesses the capability of understanding parental directives. For most children this understanding and the "testing of the waters" begins at approximately 18 to 24 months of age.

SETTING: Take the child to a private location. If at home, take him or her away from siblings, guests or other family members. In a public facility, take the child to a restroom or some place out of view.

ASSURANCE: Explain to the child that you

have a God-given role to uphold. Assure the child that your love for him or her and your high regard for the relationship make it necessary to deter defiant behavior.

APPLICATION: The spanking should be applied to the child's bottom in a firm but controlled manner with a flat open hand.

FOLLOW-UP: Reassure the child of your love.

Remember, with regard to defiance: You are too special to put up with it, your child is too special to engage in it, and your relationship is too precious to endure it.

REVIEW: PARALLELS IN PROBLEM SOLVING

CHILD'S PROBLEM	PARENT'S PROBLEM

1. The first step in either case is to focus on the feelings. The parents either identify the child's feelings or express their own feelings.

Acknowledge feelings.	*Express feelings.*

2. In both cases the parents provide understanding. With the child's problem the parents provide insight by reflective listening and good counsel. Conversely, the child understands his or her options.

Listen and reflect. Offer good counsel when appropriate.	*Give child a choice.*

3. In this phase the parents enable the child to work out his or her problem or work out their problem by following through.

Explore alternatives.   *Apply consequence.*

4. The parents convey love and confidence in the child's ability to handle the problem. Or the parents lovingly demonstrate confidence in their own abilities and roles.

Provide encouragement.   *Spank for defiant behavior.*

A FINAL THOUGHT

In 1985 my wife and I became foster parents, licensed by the state of Ohio. As a family we decided to provide care for infants prior to their adoptions. Most babies come to us directly from the hospital and are only three or four days old. It is a little ministry that supports those young women who choose life over abortion. It is an active means of living out our convictions about the sanctity of life.

Yet caring for these little ones cannot be considered a sacrifice. Although our intent is to shower each baby with love and devotion, *we* have been the recipients of the greater blessing.

Our first little boy, whom we named Robbie, was very special to us. I can honestly say I could not have loved him more if he had been my own son. Nevertheless, when he was two months and 12 days old, the social worker called to say the placement with the adoptive family would happen within two days. We will never forget the afternoon she drove away with "our" little boy, son and brother. It was very much like a death in the family. Oh, we were pleased for the adoptive parents, but we literally mourned for Robbie and still do.

One thing became very clear to me through this experience—the realization that all of our children are temporarily on loan to us. The Lord gave them life, and ultimately they will return to Him. I love them dearly, and with God's grace I am teaching them what I understand to be worthwhile and true. One day, however, I will retire from teaching. My youngsters will have grown to young adulthood, ready to enter the real world, equipped with the lessons of our years together. Prayerfully I will release my grasp, as we did with Robbie, and heed the words my mother penned in my own youth:

> *When you were plump, pink babies,*
> *your cries in the night*
> *brought me running to pat and pamper*
> *and cuddle you quiet.*
> *Scraped knees,*

bruised hearts,
people problems,
broken dreams
brought us crying to the One
who hushed us, quietly together.
Now you are gone
and your cries in the night
I leave to the Father
who comes to quiet you
and everlastingly
carry you
in His arms of love.
  Dorothy Purdy

Teach them while you can!

Section 2

Introduction

O my people, hear my teaching;
  listen to the words of my mouth.
I will open my mouth in parables,
  I will utter hidden things, things from of old—
what we have heard and known,
  what our fathers have told us.
We will not hide them from their children;
  we will tell the next generation
the praiseworthy deeds of the Lord,
  his power, and the wonders he has done.
  He decreed statutes for Jacob
  and established the law in Israel,
  which he commanded our forefathers
  to teach their children,
so the next generation would know them,
  even the children yet to be born,
  and they in turn would tell their children.
Then they would put their trust in God
  and would not forget his deeds
  but would keep his commands.
  (Psalm 78:1–7)

The Bible is certainly adamant that the truths of God should be passed on to our children. It also specifically designates fathers as the primary teachers. When a parent teaches, there are two important messages to the child.

First, the adult is saying that Scripture is important. This is essentially the message we are giving when we take our children to Sunday school. However, when I *personally* teach spiritual principles there is another very powerful message my child picks up—God's Word is important to *me*!

As delineated in the first section of this book, the extent to which a child will accept and internalize our teaching is predicated on the quality of our relationship. Assuming the realtionship is healthy, a child will profit more through his or her parents' teaching than any other source. The problem is that many of us are well meaning, but lack in the continuity and regularity of a structured teaching approach.

In this section of the book there are 12 activities and stories from Scripture to be discussed with your children on a monthly basis. Relevant concepts, verses and vocabulary words complement the teaching and can be studied weekly. Space is provided on these pages to record your personal points of discussion and the children's responses. What a joy it might be years from now to review this treasury of childhood insights. These activities will enrich and enhance your children's lives. You can encourage the application of these principles as you consciously apply them to your own life as well.

Prior to each lesson you should spend time in prayer asking God to illuminate for you the most important points of study. Next, familiarize yourself with the passage or study word and make special note of those concepts you wish to highlight. Finally, look for ways in which you can actively involve your children in a meaningful and practical way—this is especially important if you have a range of ages among your children. With older children you can actually have them lead the study on occasion.

God will bless you as you seek to honor him in this important learning experience for your children.

JANUARY

Resolutions

For the last several years we have enjoyed spending New Year's Eve at home together as a family. As we approach midnight, we discuss resolutions for the coming year. The memory of our first family New Year's Eve gathering is indelibly etched in my mind.

Ann and I asked the children to select one thing mom and dad needed to really work on in the ensuing year. The kids trotted off to the kitchen to study the matter while Ann and I remained in the living room to sort out some goals for the children.

The giggles and laughter in the kitchen made us wonder which of our inadequacies or shortcomings they were dissecting at the moment. Meanwhile, it took us no more than 60 seconds to determine our goals for Ben, Hannah and Carolyn. Assessing the obvious is not all that difficult!

When we reconvened each child was asked

to guess his or her respective New Year's resolution. The accuracy of our kids was uncanny! Without hesitation they *knew* the goals we had selected for them. Then it was my turn.

Ben, the spokesman for the group, asked me to guess my resolution. Considering all of the things I needed to work on in my role as husband and father, I made numerous incorrect guesses.

Finally Ben announced, "What we want most from you, Dad, is to keep on loving us."

I was stunned. In effect, they were saying, "We can overlook your faults, Dad, but your love for us is indispensable." I pray I'll never forget it.

This little tradition has been a wonderful experience for us. It is a time of sharing, soul-baring, trust and respect. As the year unfolds, we avoid using these resolutions as weapons of war. Needling and nagging one another would be counterproductive. Nevertheless, we do take time on occasion to review our progress.

When reviewing our objectives, I try to play the role of encourager rather than judge and jury. It is self-evaluation we are pursuing. Anyhow, I can't afford the luxury of sitting back and taking pot shots at others. After all, I have my hands full with my own resolution. Consequently, I am more interested in the child's self-assessment than handing down my critique.

Although reputation is important, what we think of ourselves is equally significant. Obviously it is healthier for a child to accomplish a task because it is right and internally rewarding than to simply impress mom and dad. This is the essence of character development—the blending of self-confidence and commitment, based upon scriptural truth.

Certainly learning principles of wisdom is crucial. As an old saying goes, "You can't stand on promises if you don't know what they are." Nevertheless, it is the application of these principles that makes the difference between wisdom and foolishness, personal depth and superficiality.

If you determine to lead your family in a similar experience, I would recommend a positive approach. For example, when stating a goal it should be phrased in a positive and respectful manner. "Stop wetting your bed" is less desirable than "Wake up dry." "Speak respectfully to your sisters" is preferable to "Stop bugging your sisters."

This family time is also an excellent opportunity to discuss your appreciation for the wise behavior your children exhibit and your devotion to them regardless of behavior. This is a time of sharing and encouragement and should not be perceived as a put-down or gripe session.

Perhaps you could make Hebrews 10:24–25 your family verses:

> And let us consider how we may spur one another on toward love and good deeds. Let us not give up meeting together, as some are in the habit of doing, but let us encourage one another—and all the more as you see the Day approaching.

This whole idea of resolution involves commitment, a concept almost obsolete in contemporary relationships. Of course, establishing a solid, personal relationship with Jesus Christ is the ultimate commitment. As a means to reinforce this concept in your children, consider the vehicle of Christian music. If you have a hymnal and perhaps a piano, electronic keyboard or guitar, teach your children and sing together some of the great hymns of consecration. Some suggestions are: *Onward Christian Soldiers, Take My Life and Let It Be, All for Jesus* or *Have Thine Own Way, Lord.*

In recent years we've enjoyed some of the contemporary Christian music by Joni Eareckson-Tada, Michael Card, Sandi Patti and others that enable us to internalize spiritual truths.

Take the time to teach some songs of faith to your children.

The space below can be used for recording the resolutions for the coming year.

Dad's Resolution: _____
_____
_____

Mom's Resolution: _____
_____
_____

_____Resolution: _____

_____Resolution: _____

_____Resolution: _____

_____Resolution: _____

Personal Notes or Comments:

_____
_____
_____
_____

Week 1 Concept: WISDOM

DEFINITION: Having or showing good judgment; the ability to judge rightly and follow the soundest course of action based on knowledge, experience and understanding; a moral rather than an intellectual quality.

USED IN CONTEXT: The young girl appreciated her grandfather's *wisdom*.

BIBLE VERSE:

"A wise son brings joy to his father,
　but a foolish son grief to his mother."
　　(Proverbs 10:1)

"The fear of the Lord is the beginning of
　wisdom,
　and knowledge of the Holy One is
　understanding."
　　(Proverbs 9:10)

DISCUSSION QUESTIONS:

1. In what ways do you demonstrate wisdom?
2. Who are the wisest adults you know? Why do you consider them wise?
3. Who are the wisest children you know? Why do you consider them to be wise?
4. Do you prefer to play with wise children or foolish children? Why?

5. If you lack wisdom, what can you do? (See James 1:5.)

6. What is the result of spending lots of time with wise people? Foolish people?

PARENT: Pray specifically that your children grasp the significance of wise thinking and wise behavior.

PARENTS' AND CHILDREN'S COMMENTS:

_____

_____

_____

_____

Week 2 Concept: EAGER

DEFINITION: Keenly desiring; wanting very much; greatly enthusiastic.

USED IN CONTEXT: The mother robin was _eager_ to return to her nest with food for her babies.

BIBLE VERSES:

"That is why I am so eager to preach the gospel also to you who are at Rome" (Romans 1:15).

"But, brothers, when we were torn away from you for a short time (in person, not in thought), out of our intense longing we made every effort to see you" (1 Thessalonians 2:17).

"But we, brethren, having been bereft of you for a short while—in person, not in spirit— were all the more eager with great desire to see your face" (Same verse, KJV).

DISCUSSION QUESTIONS:

1. What things are you eager to do this week? This year?
2. Are you more eager to read a good book or play a fun game?
3. Are you usually eager to help mom and dad? Why or why not?
4. Parent, what special things are you eager to do with your children this year?
5. What things are you eager to do for Jesus?
6. What things are you eager to ask Jesus when you see Him?

PARENT: Demonstrate a real eagerness to spend time with your children this week. Make time! One way of doing this is by keeping Sunday a family day with very few commitments other than church.

PARENTS' AND CHILDREN'S COMMENTS:

_____
_____
_____
_____

Week 3 Concept: DISCERNMENT

DEFINITION: The ability to perceive or recognize differences; the ability to judge clearly; insight.

USED IN CONTEXT: The child used great *discernment* when he decided not to play with the matches another boy had brought to school.

BIBLE VERSES:

"Teach me knowledge and good judgment
(discernment, KJV)
for I believe in your commands."
(Psalm 119:66)

"Do not be like the horse or the mule,
which have no understanding."
(Psalm 32:9a)

DISCUSSION QUESTIONS:

1. Name some children you know who use good discernment.
2. In what situations is it absolutely necessary for you to be discerning?
3. Which do you think God values more: wisdom or strength? (See Ecclesiastes 9:16.)
4. To be discerning and to act on your discernment takes a special kind of strength. Can you give an example?
5. If you need help in a situation that requires

discernment, what can you do? (See James 1:5.)

PARENT: Pray that God would give you much discernment in your family relationships.

PARENTS' AND CHILDREN'S COMMENTS:

_____

_____

_____

_____

Week 4 Concept: ENCOURAGE

DEFINITION: To give hope or confidence to; to help or give support to; be favorable to; to give courage.

USED IN CONTEXT: The little girl needed lots of _encouragement_ while she was learning to ride her bike without training wheels.

BIBLE VERSES:

"Therefore encourage one another and build each other up, just as in fact you are doing" (1 Thessalonians 5:11).

"But encourage one another daily, as long as it is called Today, so that none of you may be hardened by sin's deceitfulness" (Hebrews 3:13).

DISCUSSION QUESTIONS:

1. Who in our family gives you a lot of encouragement?

2. Name someone outside of our family who gives you lots of encouragement.

3. When someone encourages you, how does it feel?

4. Do you think other people consider you an encouraging person?

5. Name-calling and making fun of someone is discouraging. How does it feel when people treat you in a discouraging way?

6. Think of someone you can encourage this week. How will you do it?

PARENT: One of the greatest gifts we can give is the gift of encouragement.

PARENTS' AND CHILDREN'S COMMENTS:

_____

_____

_____

_____

David and Goliath

First Samuel 17

King Saul and the people of Israel were locked in combat with the armies of the Philistines. Goliath, a champion warrior of the Philistines, made a challenge to the ranks of Israel that placed the entire nation in jeopardy.

This nine-foot giant of a man, who wore armor weighing about 125 pounds, offered to fight any man in Saul's army. The losing side would from that point be in bondage to the victor. Needless to say, much was at stake and the prospects of winning were not very good. It must have looked like the Cleveland Browns swaggering into the local high school team's locker room looking for a game. The difference? This was no game! This was life and death and the future of a nation.

It is interesting that Goliath defied the armies of Israel for 40 days, the same period of time that Jesus prayed in the wilderness and the duration it rained during Noah's experience. Forty, in Scripture, often refers to a time of testing, and this was no exception.

It wasn't until a youth appeared on the scene that anyone considered taking on this fearsome foe. David, while bringing supplies to his brothers, heard Goliath's challenge and was appalled at what he saw.

"Who is this uncircumcised Philistine that he should defy the armies of the living God?" (verse 26) he said. This young man with more faith and conviction than the strongest soldiers in Saul's army was not the least bit intimidated by Goliath's strength and stature. Verses 34 through 37 explain why. You see, David's was not a blind faith. He had witnessed the Lord's faithfulness while he was confronted by a lion and a bear when tending his father's sheep. He knew that as formidable an opponent as Goliath was, "the battle is the Lord's" (verse 47).

This situation is not unlike the time when Peter walked toward Jesus on the water in Matthew 14. When Peter looked at Jesus, all was well, but the moment he began looking at the circumstances around him, he began to sink. Just when Saul's army was sinking in despair, David arrived, walking in the conviction and power of God's will.

Nevertheless, David's faith and indignation

were not initially well received by his brothers. His older brother, Eliab, accused him of being an irresponsible little kid just popping off and looking for a front row seat at the local battle. A valuable lesson kids can learn through this story is that sometimes when we stand up for what is just and right we aren't very popular, even with our friends and family.

First Timothy 4:12 is a New Testament expression of this Old Testament truth:

> Don't let anyone look down on you because you are young, but set an example for the believers in speech, in life, in love, in faith and in purity.

There will be many Goliaths in the lives of our children, but they need to be taught that greater is He who is in them than the challenges in the world. There is an old saying: it's not the size of the dog in the fight; it is the size of the fight in the dog. From a spiritual standpoint, it is not the size or fury of the foe, but the faith of the believer and the sufficiency of the Lord.

In the events surrounding David and Goliath there are three significant teaching points. (You may find more.)

> 1. No one is too young or too small to serve the Lord and be an example for others.

2. No situation is too difficult for the Lord. You can do *all* things through Jesus Christ who gives you strength (Philippians 4:13).

3. When you make a stand for what you believe to be right, it may not be popular, but popularity is not as important as living by your convictions.

PERSONAL NOTES:

_____

_____

_____

_____

Week 1 Concept: STRENGTH

DEFINITION: Force; power; the power to resist strain or stress.

USED IN CONTEXT: It took great *strength* to lift the heavy box.

BIBLE VERSES:

"Finally, be strong in the Lord and in his mighty power" (Ephesians 6:10).

"I can do everything through him who gives me strength" (Philippians 4:13).

"The Lord is the stronghold (strength, KJV) of my life—
of whom shall I be afraid?" (Psalm 27:1b).

NOTE: There are many types of strength. One type of strength takes strong muscles. It also takes strength to stand up for what you believe when others around you don't agree. It takes mental strength to fight pain and distress. You may not be physically strong, but list some other ways you can be strong.

DISCUSSION QUESTIONS:

1. What type of strength is described in Ephesians 6:10?
2. What are some ways we can demonstrate physical strength?
3. What are some ways we can show strength of character?
4. Did David (in the story of David and Goliath) demonstrate more physical strength or spiritual strength?
5. Does self-control require a type of strength? (See Proverbs 16:32.)
6. List some ways you are going to be strong this week.
7. Where can you find strength to help you accomplish these things?

PARENT: "Catch" your youngster being strong in character this week (making a wise decision, acting responsibly, making a bold statement, expressing his or her feelings appropriately). Be sure to acknowledge such to your child.

_____
_____
_____
_____

Week 2 Concept: COURAGE

DEFINITION: Bravery; fearlessness; boldness; valor.

USED IN CONTEXT: Some children have the _courage_ to do what is right, even when other kids behave foolishly.

BIBLE VERSES:

> "Be strong and courageous. Do not be afraid or terrified because of them, for the Lord your God goes with you; he will never leave you nor forsake you" (Deuteronomy 31:6).

> "Be strong and take heart (be of good courage, KJV), all you who hope in the Lord" (Psalm 31:24).

DISCUSSION QUESTIONS:

1. Can you name someone you consider to be courageous?
2. Do you have to be grown up to demonstrate courage?
3. Think of a time when you were courageous.
4. Which takes more courage: drinking a can

of beer or refusing to take the can of beer when your friend hands it to you?

5. In what ways does God expect you to be courageous?

PARENT: Have the courage to "let go" in some area this week. Allow your child the opportunity to make his or her own decision about something you previously had controled.

PARENTS' AND CHILDREN'S COMMENTS:

_____

_____

_____

_____

Week 3 Concept: OMNIPOTENT

DEFINITION: The quality of having unlimited power or authority. God can do anything He wills, but He does not will evil because of His nature. Only God is omnipotent.

USED IN CONTEXT: Becaue God is *omnipotent* He can meet our every need.

BIBLE VERSES:

"I can do everything through him who gives me strength" (Philippians 4:13).

"For nothing is impossible with God" (Luke 1:37).

"Is anything too hard for the Lord?" (Genesis 18:14a).

NOTE: Sometimes we, as people, limit God by trying to bring Him down to our size. We see Him merely as a big person. But God is all-powerful beyond our wildest imagination. And His unlimited power and love are available to us through His Spirit. (See 1 Corinthians 2:9.)

DISCUSSION QUESTIONS:

1. What are some stories you remember from the Bible that show God's omnipotence?
2. How can knowing that God is omnipotent help us when we face problems?

PARENT: Pray with your children asking God to show His omnipotence this week. For example, you might pray with the child asking God for His strength to help the child give up TV for a week, love an enemy, give a testimony in church or love someone not so loveable.

PARENTS' AND CHILDREN'S COMMENTS:

Week 4 Concept: CONFIDENCE

DEFINITION: Firm belief; trust in someone or something.

USED IN CONTEXT: I have *confidence* in your ability to handle a paper route.

BIBLE VERSES:

"It is better to take refuge in the Lord
than to trust (put confidence, KJV) in man."
(Psalm 118:8)

"Being confident of this, that he who began a good work in you will carry it on to completion until the day of Christ Jesus" (Philippians 1:6).

DISCUSSION QUESTIONS:

1. Why is Psalm 118:8 true?
2. Do you think self-confidence is important? Why?
3. Are you a confident person in most situations?
4. In which people in your life do you have the most confidence? Why?
5. What are some ways you might build your self-confidence? How can we help you? We're confident you can do it!

PARENT: Spend an evening with your child making a collage by cutting out pictures of things he or she has confidence in doing. In addition, you might want to select a picture of something your child wishes he or she had the confidence to do. Then, if possible, set up a plan to acheive that goal.

PARENTS' AND CHILDREN'S COMMENTS:

_____

_____

_____

_____

MARCH

Wisdom vs. Foolishness

Our children have enjoyed discussing wisdom and foolishness by playing the "Wise Willie, Foolish Freddie" game. In this game, I create various situations and ask the children to determine the typical response of a Foolish Freddie or the thoughful approach of a Wise Willie.

What would Foolish Freddie and Wise Willie do in the following situations?

1. You find a piece of gum on the sidewalk.
2. A strange man pulls up in a car and asks you to get in.
3. You see a neat toy in a store, but you don't have any money with you.
4. Someone touches you where you don't like to be touched and makes you promise not to tell.
5. Some kids call you names on the playground.

111

6. Some kids start smoking and offer you a cigarette.

7. You are taking a test in school and you notice some kids cheating.

8. A teacher makes a brief statement in class that is contrary to your beliefs.

9. Your dad does something that makes you angry.

10. The phone rings. Your dad say to answer it and, if it's for him, tell the caller that he's not there.

11. Your friend offers you $5.00 for your toy truck. He doesn't know the wheels come off and the axle is broken—but you do.

12. Some kids are making fun of another kid at school.

13. Your mom asks you to set the table and you don't want to do it.

14. You are playing with someone when your best friend calls and invites you over to his house.

15. Your dad offers you $1.00 for your allowance today or $2.00 if you wait until tomorrow.

16. You break the rung on a dining room chair, but it can be adjusted so the crack is not easily seen.

17. You accidentally burp in the classroom. The teacher whirls around and in anger gives a detention to the student seated next to you.

Of course it follows that we discuss the reasons behind Willie's discernment and Freddie's blunders. Freddie is a follower. He follows the crowd because peer acceptance is his primary goal. Freddie is also impulsive. He leaps before he looks. Willie may be a follower, but he knows who to follow. He has temptations common to Freddie, but he gives careful consideration to the consequences of specific behaviors. Freddie is foolish because his values are disoriented, and perhaps television and neighborhood children are the most significant influences in his life.

In Willie's life, probably his parents have the most significant influence. Oh, they make mistakes, too, but they model consistent and appropriate values for him. They take time to actively teach Willie the values and reasons for their convictions.

By nature, children are often inclined to assume the role of Foolish Freddie. It takes significant and special people in their lives to carefully teach them the importance of wise thinking and wise behavior. Mom and dad, you are those people!

A good family activity for this month is to read through the book of Proverbs—its 31 chapters make it convenient to read a chapter per day. As you read you will find Proverbs absolutely saturated with insight on wisdom and foolishness. Look for specific mention comparing wisdom and foolishness, the need to teach such lessons to children and the values God deems important.

PERSONAL NOTES:

_____
_____
_____
_____

Week 1 Concept: FOOLISH

DEFINITION: Without good sense or wisdom.

USED IN CONTEXT: The *foolish* boy crossed the busy street without looking.

BIBLE VERSES:

"A foolish son brings grief to his father
   and bitterness to the one who bore him."
      (Proverbs 17:25)

"Therefore do not be foolish, but understand what the Lord's will is" (Ephesians 5:17).

DISCUSSION QUESTIONS:

1. What are some foolish things that children your age do?
2. If you hang around with foolish children, how will that affect you? (See First Corinthians 15:33.)

3. Which person do you think is happier: one who is wise or one who is foolish?

4. Which of these traits—wisdom or foolishness—best describes you?

PARENT: Watch a TV show together as a family during which you note any evidence of foolish behavior. Compare and discuss your findings. Commercials often offer an abundance of material for discussion.

PARENTS' AND CHILDREN'S COMMENTS:

_____

_____

_____

_____

Week 2 Concept: MORAL

DEFINITION: Capable of making the distinction between right and wrong in conduct; good or right in character.

USED IN CONTEXT: The teenager was selected for the award because of her fine *moral* character.

BIBLE VERSE:

> "Do not be misled: 'Bad company corrupts good character (morals, KJV)' " (1 Corinthians 15:33).

DISCUSSION QUESTIONS:

1. According to First Corinthians 15:33, does

it matter whom we select as our friends? In what way?

2. How do we know what is right and what is wrong?

3. Do you think a four-year-old child is too young to be working on his or her morals?

PARENT: Make a list of moral behaviors and post them on the refrigerator door. Anyone observing another family member demonstrating such behavior can place a tally mark by that item on the list. Some good discussion can result from this activity.

PARENTS' AND CHILDREN'S COMMENTS:

_____

_____

_____

_____

Week 3 Concept: TRUTH

DEFINITION: Opposed to falsehood; an established or verified fact or principle; honesty; trustworthiness.

USED IN CONTEXT: Moms and dads always appreciate their children telling them the _truth_.

BIBLE VERSES:

"Jesus answered, 'I am the way and the truth

and the life. No one comes to the Father except through me' " (John 14:6).

"For the Lord is good and his love endures
    forever;
  his faithfulness (truth, KJV) continues
    through all generations."
  (Psalm 100:5)

"Your word is truth" (John 17:17).

DISCUSSION QUESTIONS:

1. Do you always tell the truth?
2. When is it difficult to tell the truth?
3. Truth in love is necessary especially between people who care for each other. Why?
4. What's the difference between being being
brutally honest and speaking the truth in love?
5. Do you believe the Bible is truth as it claims
to be?
6. If so, doesn't it make sense to you to read
what it says?

PARENT: Discuss with your children a time
when you had difficulty telling the truth. Did
you manage to come through or did you fail?
What were the consequences, and what did
you learn from this experience?

PARENTS' AND CHILDREN'S COMMENTS:

_____

_____

Week 4 Concept: TRUST

DEFINITION: Firm belief or confidence in another person or thing.

USED IN CONTEXT: "*Trust* me," the doctor said to the little boy. "I won't hurt you."

BIBLE VERSES:

> "Trust in the Lord with all your heart
>   and lean not on your own understanding;
> in all your ways acknowledge him,
>   and he will make your paths straight."
>   (Proverbs 3:5–6)

> "And again,
>   'I will put my trust in him.'
> And again he says,
>   'Here am I, and the children God has given
>   me.' "
>   (Hebrews 2:13)

DISCUSSION QUESTIONS:

1. Name the people you trust the most.
2. Do you think you are trustworthy?
3. How do people learn to trust us?
4. Does God want us to trust Him?
5. Is He trustworthy?
6. How can we best demonstrate our trust in Him?

118

PARENT: Trust your children to do something different or unusual. For example, trust them to make lunch for you. Turn off your alarm and trust them to awaken you by using their alarm clock. Go to bed early and have them lock up the house. Let them take you on a mystery hike, perhaps leading you blindfolded. Of course, the ages of your children will determine your activities.

PARENTS' AND CHILDREN'S COMMENTS:

_____

_____

_____

_____

APRIL

Jonah and the Big Fish

The nautical story of Jonah and the fish—the word *whale* is not used in Scripture—clearly illustrates the essence of God's character. The very reason He commanded Jonah to travel to the city of Nineveh tells us something about God.

First of all, God detests sin, and He was well aware of the wickedness in the city. Due to God's omnipresent nature, He is cognizant of all things at all times, so He knew about Nineveh. Personally, we need to understand that our heavenly Father's righteous nature is to desire righteousness in our lives.

Although we don't want to paint the picture of an ominous figure hovering above waiting to pounce on our every mistake, God is interested in and fully cognizant of our attitudes and behavior.

Yet God also reveals His wonderful quality of compassion. He loves each of us "without respect of persons," even as He loved the evil people of Nineveh.

What God is saying in this book is what we tell our own children. We may hate what they have done—the sin—but we love them—the sinners. Our love separates the action from the child who did it. Although Jonah vehemently disdains the people from Nineveh in a condescending way, God shows His great compassion for the people and even the animals of that city.

While Jonah depicts the nature of man as he selfishly neglects this sinful but needy people, God tells us to recognize our sin, turn from it and He will lovingly forgive us, just as He did the dreaded Ninevites. Jonah wanted God to destroy Nineveh. God was determined to save it.

It is interesting that from the time Jonah disobeys God his life is headed downhill. Consequences for disobedience are inevitable as Galatians 6:7 explains, "Do not be deceived: God is not mocked. A man reaps what he sows." When Jonah fled to Tarshish thinking he could run from God, he went *down* to Joppa, *down* to the ship headed for Tarshish, *down* below into the hold of the ship and he lay *down.* In time he would be *down* in the belly of a fish in the depths of the sea. The moral of the story—disobedience will bring you *down.*

Furthermore, foolish behavior brings down all those around you as well. All the men in the ship headed to Tarshish were in jeopardy due to one man's actions. We do not live in a vacuum, away from others. A common retort heard today is "what I do is no one else's business" or "I'm only hurting myself." That simply isn't true. Smoking has detrimental side effects upon nonsmokers; the AIDS virus can be transmitted through blood transfusions; pro-choice leaves the baby no choice; and the child of an alcoholic suffers due to the sickness of the parent.

In the book of Jonah there are several good teaching points for children.

1. God is omnipresent. He is everywhere at all times.
2. God is omniscient. He has unlimited knowledge and is intimately acquainted with all our ways.
3. God is compassionate. He loves us even when we are not loveable. That is *the* perfect love.

PERSONAL NOTES:

_____

_____

Week 1 Concept: OMNISCIENT

DEFINITION: The ability of infinite knowledge; knowing everything past, present and future. Only God is omniscient.

USED IN CONTEXT: Because God is *omniscient*, He knows everything about us.

BIBLE VERSES:

> "Would not God have discovered it,
>   since he knows the secrets of the heart?"
>   (Psalm 44:21)

> "For the eyes of the Lord range throughout the earth" (2 Chronicles 16:9a).

> "Great is our Lord and mighty in power;
>   his understanding has no limit."
>   (Psalm 147:5)

NOTE: God knows everything about you. (See Matthew 10:29.) Not only does God know all about you, but He personally loves you very much. (See First John 3:16 and First Peter 5:6–7.)

DISCUSSION QUESTIONS:

1. James 1:17 states, "Every good and perfect gift is from above." How special are you in God's creation?

2. How should the fact that God knows everything we do and say affect the way we live?

PARENT: Since God knows everything, discuss some of the questions you'd like to ask God.

PARENTS' AND CHILDREN'S COMMENTS:

_____

_____

_____

_____

Week 2 Concept: OMNIPRESENT

DEFINITION: Present in all places at the same time; ubiquitous. Only God is omnipresent.

USED IN CONTEXT: Because God is _omnipresent_, He can be everyplace at the same time.

BIBLE VERSES:

> " 'Can anyone hide in secret places
>   so that I cannot see him?'
>   declares the Lord.
> 'Do I not fill heaven and earth?'
>   declares the Lord."
>   (Jeremiah 23:24)

> "The eyes of the Lord are everywhere,
>   keeping watch on the wicked and the good."
>   (Proverbs 15:3)

> "Where can I go from your Spirit?
>   Where can I flee from your presence?"

(Psalm 139:7)

NOTE: This is a difficult concept for us to understand. Note that Jesus said it was better for us that He leave the earth in bodily form for this reason. (See John 16.)

DISCUSSION QUESTIONS:

1. Isn't it a comfort to know that the Lord, through His Spirit, is always with you? (See Matthew 28:19–20.)
2. Name some ways that His omnipresence is a comfort to us.

PARENT: Discuss a time when God's presence was very real to you.

PARENTS' AND CHILDREN'S COMMENTS:

_____

_____

_____

_____

Week 3 Concept: OBEY

DEFINITION: To carry out the instructions or orders of; submit to the control of. The crowning test of faith in God is obedience.

USED IN CONTEXT: It makes parents happy when their children *obey* them.

"This is how we know that we love the children of God: by loving God and carrying out his commands" (1 John 5:2).

"Children, obey your parents in the Lord, for this is right" (Ephesians 6:1).

DISCUSSION QUESTIONS:

1. When the Bible says to obey your parents, it then gives a promise. Do you know what it says? (See Exodus 20:12.)

2. The Bible also says that God desires obedience more than sacrifice. What does this mean? (See First Samuel 15:22.)

3. Are you obedient to your parents all of the time, most of the time, some of the time or none of the time?

4. When is it most difficult to obey?

PARENT: Remember, as we enable our children to learn about obedience, the lesson is more readily accepted when we refrain from provoking our children to anger.

PARENTS' AND CHILDREN'S COMMENTS:

_____
_____
_____
_____

Week 4 Concept: VIGILANT

DEFINITION: Watchful; alert to danger.

USED IN CONTEXT: The doe was ever *vigilant* and protective of her fawn.

BIBLE VERSES:

> "Be self-controled and alert (vigilant, KJV). Your enemy the devil prowls around like a roaring lion looking for someone to devour" (1 Peter 5:8).

> "Therefore keep watch, because you do not know on what day your Lord will come" (Matthew 24:42).

> "Let the wise listen and add to their learning, and let the discerning get guidance." (Proverbs 1:5)

DISCUSSION QUESTIONS:

1. In what ways do we need to be vigilant?
2. The opposite of vigilant is oblivious or negligent. Which word best describes you— vigilant or negligent?
3. Why is it necessary to be vigilant?

PARENT: Being alert to the obvious is not that difficult. When you hear a siren on the road you pull over. When you see a thunderstorm approach you take cover. When you see your toddler about to topple down the basement

127

stairs you step in to avert the problem. But what about more subtle dangers? The media portray alcohol, sex and violence in such attractive packages. Heavy metal music is not the least bit subtle, but are you aware of its messages? Matthew 12:29 says, "How can anyone enter a strong man's house and carry off his possessions unless he first ties up the strong man?" We must be strong and vigilant as parents because our homes are filled with treasure more precious than property.

PARENTS' AND CHILDREN'S COMMENTS:

_____

_____

_____

_____

MAY

Daniel and the Lions' Den

Daniel 1–6

When Daniel was still in his youth, Israel was placed in captivity by the Babylonians. God, however, used Daniel to teach Nebuchadnezzar, the king of Babylon, the reality of the one true God.

Although he was a child of Israel, Daniel was brought up in the king's court shortly after his deportation to Babylon. Prior to this deportation it is obvious that Daniel was strongly influenced in his faith by Israel's good king Josiah and the teachings of Jeremiah.

Daniel was about 70 years old when the incident occurred in the lions' den. Therefore, the truths he learned as a boy remained strongly entrenched—to the point of death—for almost 60 years. What a message to us as parents! There are young "Daniels" in our homes watching and learning from us.

As a young man Daniel grew in favor with King Nebuchadnezzar. He held a high administrative office with both the Babylonians and the Persians. Yet his strong but simple faith remained intact and his life was a shining example of humility and godliness. Despite all of this, his status never went to his head. He is one of very few men about whom God had only positive things to say. God refers to Daniel as His "greatly beloved," much like his counterpart, John, in the New Testament.

God gave Daniel the gift of prophecy and the ability to interpret dreams. This ability was one of the things that endeared him to the nobility of that day. Furthermore, it was Daniel's moral courage that made those around him take notice. He not only refused to defile himself with the king's meat and wine, he chose the den of lions rather than renounce his daily prayer life. In essence, he was serving in an earthly court, but his allegiance was unquestionably and totally to the God of Israel.

For each of us today it is a lesson of living *in* the world, but not being *of* the world. Daniel didn't attempt to isolate himself in some Jewish commune. He worked in the hub of a secular kingdom, like many of us do today. Nevertheless, it was through Daniel that Nebuchadnezzar proclaimed to the world his acknowledgement of Israel's God. It wasn't merely Daniel's supernatural achievements, but the strength of his character that influenced the king. How important our example and lifestyle can be!

At the time of Darius's reign, Daniel had become a commissioner, one of only three in the kingdom. His job was to oversee the satraps—or governors—and he was distinguishing himself in an amazing way. Although the other governmental officials were jealous of Daniel's accomplishments, they could find no reason to indict him due to his faithfulness and diligence. Therefore they attempted to set him up by spiritual means. In Daniel 6:10, even though he was aware of his predicament, Daniel remained unwavering in his prayer life. As we read on we find that it is Daniel's spiritual faithfulness that eventually opens up the kingdom for religious freedom. If Daniel had submitted, it would have had major implications for all of the people of that day.

Darius was obviously perplexed by the dilemma and spent a sleepless night fasting over the matter. In verse 16, Darius makes an interesting comment: "May your God, whom you serve continually, rescue you!" I guess real faithfulness is contagious! Of course, God comes through and binds the lions' mouths—a relief to both Daniel and Darius.

Daniel's malicious accusers *and* their families are thrown to the lions and instantly devoured. Our families suffer when the parents' lives run contrary to God's principles! The conniving commissioners virtually led their wives and children right into the pit.

Here are some teaching points for the children:

1. Despite our age or position in life we can be a vital witness for our Lord.
2. God honors those who honor Him. (See First Samuel 2:30.)
3. Jealousy and wicked scheming result in destruction.
4. God hears the prayers of the righteous and delights in the faithful.
5. Our spiritual walk as parents is so important that the well being of our family is often contingent upon it.
6. We live in the world, but we should not be *of* the world.

PERSONAL NOTES:

_____

_____

_____

_____

_____

_____

Week 1 Concept: *ENDURANCE*

DEFINITION: The ability to stand pain, distress or fatigue; the ability to last, continue, remain or tolerate.

USED IN CONTEXT: The long-distance runner had great *endurance* as she finished the five-mile run in record time.

BIBLE VERSES:

"Consider it pure joy, my brothers, whenever you face trials of many kinds, because you know that the testing of your faith develops perseverance (endurance, KJV). Perseverance must finish its work so that you may be mature and complete, not lacking anything" (James 1:2–4).

"[Love] always perseveres (endures, KJV)" (1 Corinthians 13:7b).

DISCUSSION QUESTIONS:

1. In what ways does a young boy or girl need to develop endurance?
2. In what ways do parents need to exhibit endurance?
3. Why does a Christian need to develop endurance?

PARENT: This would be an ideal time to read the story about the tortoise and the hare as you discuss the implications of the Christian life.

PARENTS' AND CHILDREN'S COMMENTS:

_____

_____

_____

_____

Week 2 Concept: WORSHIP

DEFINITION: To have intense love or admiration for; extreme devotion; homage rendered to God.

USED IN CONTEXT: The little children *worshiped* the Lord with prayers and songs of praise.

BIBLE VERSES:

"Come, let us bow down in worship,
   let us kneel before the Lord our Maker."
      (Psalm 95:6)

"Worship the Lord your God and serve him only" (Luke 4:8).

"At the name of Jesus every knee should bow" (Philippians 2:10b).

NOTE: It is important to worship as a family, with other believers and individually.

DISCUSSION QUESTIONS:

1. What type of family worship do you enjoy?

2. How often do you worship together?

3. How often do you worship by yourself?

4. Name some reasons why God is worthy of our praise.

PARENT: Do you have a regularly scheduled family devotion time where you pray openly together? Perhaps you could teach your children the various aspects of prayer, which include worship, requests, seeking forgiveness and thanksgiving. (See Philippians 4:6.)

PARENTS' AND CHILDREN'S COMMENTS:

_____

_____

_____

_____

Week 3 Concept: DILIGENCE

DEFINITION: Hardworking; done with careful, steady effort.

USED IN CONTEXT: She showed *diligence* in completing her homework assignments.

BIBLE VERSES:

"Let us not become weary in doing good, for at the proper time we will reap a harvest if we do not give up" (Galatians 6:9).

"Be devoted to one another in brotherly love. Honor one another above yourselves. Never be lacking in zeal (diligence, KJV), but keep your spiritual fervor, serving the Lord" (Romans 12:10–11).

"If a man will not work, he shall not eat" (2 Thessalonians 3:10b).

DISCUSSION QUESTIONS:

1. In what areas of your life is it necessary to be diligent?
2. Do you know someone who is diligent?
3. Is there a certain area of your life in which you need to become more diligent?
4. If a farmer is not diligent in harvesting his crops, what might happen?

NOTE: Remember, for your life to be fruitful you need to be diligent in the work of the Lord.

PARENT: Philippians 2:14 states: "Do everything without complaining or arguing." I would imagine that includes household chores as well.

PARENTS' AND CHILDREN'S COMMENTS:

_____

_____

_____

_____

Week 4 Concept: *ZEALOUS*

DEFINITION: Ardently devoted to a purpose; eagerly interested and enthusiastic.

USED IN CONTEXT: Some of the children were not interested in spiritual matters, but one child was *zealous* for the Lord.

BIBLE VERSES:

> "Who gave himself for us to redeem us from all wickedness and to purify for himself a people that are his very own, eager (zealous, KJV) to do what is good" (Titus 2:14).

> "He replied, 'I have been very zealous for the Lord God Almighty' " (1 Kings 19:10a).

DISCUSSION QUESTIONS:

1. If someone was zealous for the Lord, how would they behave?
2. Do you have zeal and enthusiasm for any particular thing?
3. What is the opposite of a zealous person? (See Proverbs 26:13–15.)

PARENT: Consider reading the children a biography of a person zealously commited to the Lord's work. Check you church library or local Christian bookstore for ideas. A chapter per night would be a meaningful way to end the day.

PARENTS' AND CHILDREN'S COMMENTS:

_____

_____

_____

_____

JUNE

Family Skit

To bring scriptural principles to life, consider using family skits or Christian drama. Our family has enjoyed reading various Bible stories, which we have ad-libbed afterward.

Each member selects a part. In the case of the prodigal son the skit can be performed with any number of participants. The prodigal son and the father are the two essential roles, but you might have a narrator, the older brother, the servants and even a pig or two and the fatted calf.

You should allow your children to select their choice of parts even if it means assuming an adult role. A six-year-old can enjoy playing the father while a parent becomes the son. Some real insight can be gained from role reversals.

When doing the skit the text need not be quoted verbatim. If necessary read the story through several times so that everyone feels comfortable with the essence of the script. Then act it out. Your children will enjoy this activity and the stories and truths of Scripture will take on a deeper meaning. To reinforce the lesson you might want to discuss the feelings each actor experienced during the course of the skit. For example, if you did the prodigal son, how did the father feel when his son took his inheritance prematurely? Did he expect things would work out well for his son? Was it difficult for the father to let him go? How did the son feel when he ended up eating slop with the pigs? How did the father feel when he saw his son returning home? How did the son feel when his father lovingly welcomed him home? How did the older brother feel and why? What is the real meaning of this parable? How does it apply to *your* life?

Below is a list of Bible stories and parables with respective references. These make good skits for families. Use your imagination! Be creative and enjoy the experience.

THE PRODIGAL SON (Luke 15): The love and forgiveness of our Father despite our own foolishness.

DAVID AND GOLIATH (1 Samuel 17): The strength and faithfulness of a boy and God.

DANIEL AND THE LIONS' DEN (Daniel 6): The strength and faithfulness of Daniel and God.

JONAH AND THE GREAT FISH (Jonah): The importance of obedience.

NOAH AND THE ARK (Genesis 6–9): Obedience in the midst of persecution.

SHADRACH, MESCHACH AND ABEDNEGO (Daniel 3): Strength and faithfulness in the midst of danger.

RUTH AND NAOMI (Ruth 1): Loyalty.

MARY AND MARTHA (Luke 10): Priorities.

PETER AND JESUS WALKING ON THE WATER (Matthew 14): Trust and focus on the Lord.

JESUS WASHING THE DISCIPLES' FEET (John 13): Serving one another.

ABRAHAM AND ISAAC (Genesis 22): Obedience and trust.

JOSEPH AND HIS COAT OF MANY COLORS (Genesis 37): All things work together for good.

SAMSON AND DELILAH (Judges 16): Resisting temptation.

FEEDING OF THE 5,000 (John 6): The power of God.

ADAM, EVE AND THE SERPENT (Genesis 3): Obedience.

ZACCHEUS'S CONVERSION (Luke 19): God's love

for sinners and repentance.

BUILDING YOUR HOUSE ON THE ROCK (Matthew 7): Being grounded in the Word.

THE UNMERCIFUL SLAVE (Matthew 18): Forgiveness.

THE LOST SHEEP (Luke 15): Everyone is special in God's eyes.

THE GOOD SAMARITAN (Luke 10): Good neighbor policy.

THE BANQUET (Luke 14): Responding to God's calling.

THE TALENTS (Matthew 25): Wise investment of your abilities and resources.

THE JUDGE (Luke 18): Persistence.

THE BIRTH OF JESUS (Luke 2): Christmas.

MOSES AND THE PLAGUES (Exodus 7–11): The power of God.

JESUS CALMS THE STORM (Mark 6): Trust in the power of the Lord.

THE TEMPTATION OF JESUS IN THE WILDERNESS (Matthew 4): Resisting evil and temptation.

GOD SPEAKS TO SAMUEL (1 Samuel 3): Being sensitive to God's call.

THE RICH YOUNG RULER (Matthew 19): Submission to God.

THE PARABLE OF THE SOWER (Mark 4): Receiving the Word.

THE MAN THROUGH THE ROOF (Luke 5): Man's persistence and God's healing power.

These are just a few of the Bible stories and parables that lend themselves to good family skits. You might also choose to use the message of a particular Bible story and adapt it to modern times. The following is a brief skit my family modified from the unmerciful slave story in Matthew 18. Ours uses the theme of forgiveness and treating others the way you would like to be treated.

SCENE 1

Once upon a time in the village of Real Life, on a playground in the middle of town, sat a big boy named Sam. Aaron, another boy in town, comes walking by.

SAM: Hi, Aaron! How ya doing?

AARON: Hi, Sam. Pretty good. What's on your mind?

SAM: Well, I was wondering if I could borrow your ball glove. I've got a big game coming up and I could really use it.

AARON: Well, I really need it, too.

SAM: Yes, I know. But I'll have it back to you by this afternoon.

143

AARON: OK, but I need it back by four o'clock.
SAM: Thanks a lot, Aaron.
Aaron walks away.

SCENE 2

In marches Lynn and her little sister Anna.
LYNN: Hi, Sam, I'm glad I found you.
SAM: What for?
LYNN: Well, Anna and I are in a talent show today and we need to borrow your yo-yo.
SAM: Beat it, squirt!
LYNN: But we have a good chance to win a prize if we only had a yo-yo.
SAM: OK, but I get half of the prize, and I want my yo-yo back by four o'clock.
LYNN: OK. Thanks, Sam.
SAM: Get lost, squirt!

SCENE 3

NARRATOR: Later that day at four o'clock, Aaron comes looking for his ball glove.
AARON: Hey, Sam, I need my ball glove now.
SAM: But I still need it.
AARON: It's four o'clock and you said that you would be finished with it by now.
SAM: I know, but couldn't you just let me keep it until tomorrow?
AARON: Sure, I guess so.
SAM: Gee, thanks! You're a pal, Aaron!
Aaron leaves.

SCENE 4

Lynn and Anna come walking by on their way to the talent show.

SAM: Hey you little squirts! Where's my yo-yo? Give it to me!

LYNN: But the talent show starts in a few minutes and we haven't used it yet.

SAM: Who cares? You said you'd have it back to me by four o'clock and it's already 4:15.

LYNN: Please, Sam. It begins in a few minutes.

SAM: No way! (He grabs the yo-yo and walks out leaving the girls crying.)

Aaron enters.

AARON: What's the matter?

GIRLS: Sam took his yo-yo away after he said we could use it in the talent show.

AARON: That guy—and after I just gave him a whole extra day to use my glove.

SCENE 5

Aaron catches up with Sam.

AARON: Hey, Sam! I understand you took the yo-yo away from the girls before they could use it for the talent show.

SAM: Who me?

AARON: Don't give me that "who me" stuff. I gave you an extra day with my glove and you turn around and hurt the girls. I'm taking the glove back and giving your yo-yo to the girls.

145

SAM: Oh no! Now what am I going to do?

QUESTIONS:

1. Which person in the skit was foolish and not kind? Why?
2. Which person was wise and kind?
3. Which person are you most like?
4. Which characters had their feelings hurt?
5. What can we learn from the skit?

PERSONAL NOTES:

_____

_____

_____

_____

Week 1 Concept: ARROGANT

DEFINITION: Full of pride and self-importance; haughty.

USED IN CONTEXT: That *arrogant* kid is a show-off. He thinks he's better than everyone else.

BIBLE VERSES:

"Let another praise you, and not your own
     mouth;
   someone else, and not your own lips."
   (Proverbs 27:2)

"Do not keep talking so proudly
   or let your mouth speak such arrogance,
for the Lord is a God who knows,

and by him deeds are weighed."
(1 Samuel 2:3)

DISCUSSION QUESTIONS:

1. What is the difference between taking pride in what you do and being arrogant?
2. How does the Lord feel about arrogance?
3. Do you know an arrogant person? If so, is that person fun to be around?
4. If you are really good at something, where does this talent come from? (See James 1:17.)

PARENT: It is important to get across the idea that every person is special in God's sight because they were created in His own image. You and your children have reason to be happy because God made no mistake when He made you. But considering James 1:17, God deserves the glory for everything. It's important to teach our children that they need to praise the Lord for all good things, not boast in themselves and what they can do. Be careful not to confuse arrogance with confidence.

PARENTS' AND CHILDREN'S COMMENTS:

_____
_____
_____
_____

Week 2 Concept: *AVARICE*

DEFINITION: Too much desire to get and keep money; greed for riches.

USED IN CONTEXT: The greedy man was known for his *avarice.*

BIBLE VERSES:

> "For the love of money is a root of all kinds of evil. Some people, eager for money, have wandered from the faith and pierced themselves with many griefs" (1 Timothy 6:10).

> "A greedy man brings trouble to his family" (Proverbs 15:27a).

DISCUSSION QUESTIONS:

1. Why is avarice a poor character trait?
2. What should our attitude be toward money and material things?
3. What is a good way to budget your money?
4. Can you think of a word that is opposite of avarice?
5. Think of a way you can demonstrate that avarice is not one of your characteristics. Apply it this week.
6. A sponge is a plantlike sea animal that can absorb many times its own weight in water. Some people are like sponges—the more they get, the more they want. Do you know any "spongy" people? Do you think they are very

happy?

PARENT: Materialism is a problem that plagues many North Americans. It will be very difficult to teach our children about avarice and greed if we are materialistic ourselves!

PARENTS' AND CHILDREN'S COMMENTS:

_____

_____

_____

_____

Week 3 Concept: HOSPITABLE

DEFINITION: Entertaining guests in a friendly, generous manner.

USED IN CONTEXT: We enjoyed visiting their family because they were so nice and *hospitable.*

BIBLE VERSES:

> "Offer hospitality to one another without grumbling. Each one should use whatever gift he has received to serve others, faithfully administering God's grace in its various forms" (1 Peter 4:9–10).

> "Do not forget to entertain (be hospitable, KJV) strangers, for by so doing some people have entertained angels without knowing it" (Hebrews 13:2).

1. List some ways you can be hospitable.

2. Who would you like to demonstrate your hospitality to this week? (Parents, you can clearly demonstrate hospitality if you all decide to invite someone from church over to dinner. Think particularly of someone who might suffer from loneliness—a widow, widower or other single person.)

PARENT: Make the distinction between being hospitable to strangers in your presence and being vulnerable to strangers in your absence.

PARENTS' AND CHILDREN'S COMMENTS:

_____

_____

_____

_____

Week 4 Concept: PATIENCE

DEFINITION: The ability to wait or endure without complaint.

USED IN CONTEXT: The little girl waited *patiently* for her turn on the swing.

BIBLE VERSES:

> "Let us not become weary in doing good, for at the proper time we will reap a harvest if we do not give up" (Galatians 6:9).

"Be patient with everyone" (1 Thessalonians 5:14b).

"Therefore, since we are surrounded by such a great cloud of witnesses, let us throw off everything that hinders and the sin that so easily entangles, and let us run with perseverance (patience, KJV) the race marked out for us" (Hebrews 12:1).

DISCUSSION QUESTIONS:

1. Sometimes it's not easy for children or parents to be patient. Name a situation this last week in which you were not very patient. (Here is a place to strengthen the concept of forgiveness. If any situations mentioned require apologies, see that they're made—even if you, parents, need to ask forgiveness.)

2. In what situations do you need to be more patient?

PARENT: This is one virtue that commonly eludes every parent from time to time. It might be wise to acknowledge this struggle to your children and to ask their patience with you.

PARENTS' AND CHILDREN'S COMMENTS:

_____

_____

_____

_____

JULY

Secular or Spiritual

You may not possess the humor of Bill Cosby
or the insight of James Dobson. Your theologi-
cal status may not measure up to Billy
Graham, and Judge Wapner may be far more
decisive than you. Your saga will most likely
be excluded from *Stories of Great Christians*. (I
always figured if they produced a series *Stories
of Mediocre Christians* I had a chance.) Nevertheless, in your child's book of *Who's Who* you
are most definitely Numero Uno.

God has selected you to be the most important and influential person in your child's life.
Despite this, our children are continually confronted with ideas and value systems that are
diametrically opposed to those we embrace, for
society's view of truth and wisdom seldom cor-
relates positively with Scripture. The majority
of people don't view the Bible as truth and our
various societal institutions reflect divergent
thinking. However, truth is truth whether we

choose to believe it or not. If a toddler fails to regard a warning about the stove being hot, it does not reduce the temperature of the stove. Even so, disregarding the veracity of the Bible does not preempt its authority. In John 17:17, Jesus states: "Sanctify them by the truth; your word is truth."

As Christians we live in the world, but we are not to be of or like the world. It is necessary to recognize the difference. In order to teach wisdom to our children we have to be clear in our own thinking.

The following are some contrasting positions of the world's view and the scriptural view. As you review them, consider where you stand, because parental understanding and commitment to truth is a prerequisite for teaching it to children.

World View	*Scriptural View*
I am an insignificant person; just a cog in a wheel, a brick in a wall.	"Are not five sparrows sold for two pennies? Yet not one of them is forgotten by God. Indeed, the very hairs on your head are numbered. Don't be afraid; you are worth more than many sparrows" (Luke 12:6–7).

Rules are made for others, not for me.	"Discipline your son and he will give you peace;/ he will bring delight to your soul./ Where there is no revelation, the people cast off restraint;/ but blessed is he who keeps the law" (Proverbs 29:17–18).
Hurt others, as you feel hurt.	"You have heard that it was said, 'Love you neighbor and hate your enemy.' But I tell you: Love your enemies and pray for those who persecute you" (Matthew 5:43–44).
There are no right or wrong values. It's up to the individual, and if left to themselves kids make wise decisions.	"There is a way that seems right to a man,/ but in the end it leads to death" (Proverbs 14:12).
There are many roads to heaven.	"Jesus answered, 'I am the way and the truth and the life. No one comes to the Father except through me' " (John 14:6).

There is no God.	"The fool has said in his heart,/ 'There is no God' " (Psalm 14:1a).
Man evolved from apes.	"And the Lord God formed man from the dust of the ground and breathed into his nostrils the breath of life, and man became a living being" (Genesis 2:7).
Babies inside the womb are not as worthwhile as babies outside the womb, thus making abortion all right.	"For you created my inmost being;/ you knit me together in my mother's womb./ I praise you because I am fearfully and wonderfully made;/ your works are wonderful,/ I know that full well./ My frame was not hidden from you/ when I was made in the secret place./ When I was woven together in the depths of the earth,/ your eyes saw my unformed body./ All the days ordained for me/ were

written in your book/ before one of them came to be" (Psalm 139:13–16).

Mentally and physically impared children are not worthwhile.

"But the Lord said to Samuel, 'Do not consider his appearance or his height, for I have rejected him. The Lord does not look at the things man looks at. Man looks at the outward appearance, but the Lord looks at the heart' " (1 Samuel 16:7).

Don't worry, those people will never influence me.

"Do not be misled: 'Bad company corrupts good character' " (1 Corinthians 15:33).

If it feels good, do it.

"How can a young man keep his way pure?/ By living according to your word" (Psalm 199:9).

No one can tell me what to do.

"A fool spurns his father's discipline,/ but whoever heeds correction shows prudence" (Proverbs 15:5).

I am more important than others. Look out for number one.	"Do not be wise in your own eyes;/ fear the Lord and shun evil./ This will bring health to your body/ and nourishment to your bones" (Proverbs 3:7–8).
I am not capable.	"I can do everything through him who gives me strength" (Philippians 4:13).
"Toot your own horn." "The squeaky wheel gets the grease."	"As it is written, 'Let him who boasts boast in the Lord' " (1 Corinthians 1:30).
Who needs Christianity? It's just a crutch anyhow. I can handle things just fine without God.	"Do you see a man wise in his own eyes?/ There is more hope for a fool than for him" (Proverbs 26:12).

Consider this passage from First Corinthians 2:12–16:

> We have not received the spirit of the world but the Spirit who is from God, that we may understand what God has freely given us. This is what we speak, not in words taught us by human wisdom but in words taught by the Spirit, expressing spiritual truths in spiritual

words. The man without the Spirit does not accept the things that come from the Spirit of God, for they are foolishness to him, and he cannot understand them, because they are spiritually discerned. The spiritual man makes judgments about all things, but he himself is not subject to any man's judgment:

"For who has known the mind of the Lord that he may instruct him?"

PERSONAL NOTES:

_____

_____

_____

_____

Week 1 Concept: NAIVE

DEFINITION: Foolishly simple; childlike; unsophisticated.

USED IN CONTEXT: The *naive* little girl believed a story older kids were telling her. She didn't realize they were just making it up to tease her.

BIBLE VERSE:

"A simple (naive, KJV) man believes anything, but a prudent man gives thought to his steps"
(Proverbs 14:15).

DISCUSSION QUESTIONS:

1. What is the difference between being pure

in heart and being naive?

2. Which does God want us to be?

3. How could you get into trouble if you were totally naive?

4. If we lack wisdom, what should we do? (See James 1:5.)

PARENT: There is a subtle, yet real difference between purity and naivete. We want our children to be wise but not necessarily "streetwise," innocent but not gullible. Pray for discerning children who are pure in heart.

PARENTS' AND CHILDREN'S COMMENTS:

_____

_____

_____

_____

Week 2 Concept: DECEIT

DEFINITION: A lie; dishonest action or trick; making a person believe what is not true.

USED IN CONTEXT: The *deceitful* man charged the little girl 50 cents for a 35-cent candy bar.

BIBLE VERSES:

"My lips will not speak wickedness,
  and my tongue will utter no deceit."
    (Job 27:4)

"Food gained by fraud (deceit, KJV) tastes

sweet to a man,
   but he ends up with a mouth full of gravel."
   (Proverbs 20:17)

DISCUSSION QUESTIONS:

1. Is it important to be trustworty? Why?
2. Can you trust someone who is deceitful?
3. It is not always easy to be honest, but it is
never good to be deceitful. Are you a trustworthy person?

PARENT: Be careful not to emulate deceitful
behavior by:
• Telling your children to notify a phone caller
that you're not home.
• Lying about the age of a child to get a less expensive ticket.
• Ignoring traffic laws.
• Purposely not mentioning problems with
your car to a potential buyer.
• Failing to return money to the cashier when
she's given you excess change.

PARENTS' AND CHILDREN'S COMMENTS:

_____
_____
_____
_____

Week 3 Concept: CONSCIENCE

DEFINITION: That faculty of the mind, or inborn sense of right or wrong, by which we judge the moral character of human conduct; a knowledge or feeling of right and wrong.

USED IN CONTEXT: It bothered his *conscience* when he stole the book.

BIBLE VERSES:

"We are sure that we have a clear conscience and desire to live honorably in every way" (Hebrews 13:18).

"Paul looked straight at the Sanhedrin and said, 'My brothers, I have fulfilled my duty to God in all good conscience to this day' " (Acts 23:1).

DISCUSSION QUESTIONS:

1. When does your conscience bother you?
2. Do you think it is good to have a conscience?
3. Can you think of a time when your conscience told you something was right or wrong?
4. Do you listen to or ignore your conscience?

PARENT: A conscience is formed early in life by means of the bonding process. Eye contact, touch, smiles, motion, cuddling, conversation and food are instrumental in this bonding relationship. During the first several months of life the conscience is developed by internalizing an adult figure. If you have a baby at home or are expecting soon, remember that early stimulation produces alertness, trust and a functional conscience.

PARENTS' AND CHILDREN'S COMMENTS:

_____

_____

_____

_____

Week 4 Concept: IGNORANCE

DEFINITION: Lack of knowledge, education or experience.

USED IN CONTEXT: Don't use *ignorance* of the law as an excuse for not following the rules.

BIBLE VERSES:

> "We do not want you to be uniformed (ignorant, KJV), brothers, about the hardships we suffered in the province of Asia" (2 Corinthians 1:8).

> "Since they did not know (were ignorant of, KJV) the righteousness that comes from God and sought to establish their own, they did not submit to God's righteousness" (Romans 10:3).

DISCUSSION QUESTIONS:

1. Of what, according to Scripture, is modern society ignorant?

2. Why is it ignorant to think we can be good without God?

PARENT: Romans 10:3 really speaks about the mentality of today's society. It is important to get your kids to understand that even though we have tremendous technology and apparent intelligence, if we reject God and His infinite wisdom, love and power, it is nothing short of ignorance.

PARENTS' AND CHILDREN'S COMMENTS:

_____

_____

_____

_____

AUGUST

The Prodigal Son

Luke 15:10–32

This is the story of a foolish son and his wise, loving father. As you and your children read these verses together keep in mind that *prodigal* means wasteful. This wayward son indulged himself and wasted his inheritance. Somehow he had failed to learn about the value of careful spending and straight living as a youngster. At the time he demanded his share of the inheritance, it was obvious to his father that no parental advice would prevent this frivolous journey. I can only imagine how much faith it must have taken for that father to abstain from following the boy or intervening in some fashion.

Eventually the young man did wise up, however. How? "But no one gave him anything," verse 16 explains. As a result, verse 17 tells us, "he came to his senses." A good lesson for loving parents! Children often learn best from the consequences of their own decisions. Sometimes we have to prayerfully stand back and let them learn in the "school of hard knocks."

So often young adults complain about the difficulty they have "getting it together." Actually, "getting it together" is simply behaving responsibly. It is unfortunate when they fail to "get it together" during childhood with the support of their loving family. In the case of the prodigal son it took a pig pen and extreme poverty to straighten him out.

You might ask your children if they think this son was a fast or a slow learner. Discuss with them the benefits of learning lessons early in life. Ask them if they would prefer to be a fast learner who avoids pig pens or one who inevitably suffers in the mire of slow learning. Your challenge, mom and dad, is to teach responsible behavior by allowing the consequences of slow learning to have impact in the formative years. In other words, it is important to let your children learn from their mistakes instead of always bailing them out.

The father in this story illustrates how God wonderfully forgives His wayward children. In a similar way we must be willing to forgive the members of our family when wrongs are committed. Digging up the past with a derogatory "I told you so" serves no good purpose.

Of course, the son returned home with a repentant heart, which is necessary for forgiveness. Verse 21 states, "Father, I have sinned against heaven and against you. I am no longer worthy to be called your son." This attitude serves as a model for each of us. When our children make mistakes—and they will because children always make mistakes—they need to be taught that genuine remorse on their part will always result in loving forgiveness on our part. This parallels our relationship with the heavenly Father.

Another issue presented in this parable involves the selfish spirit of the older brother. The Bible says, "If anyone says, 'I love God,' yet hates his brother, he is a liar. For anyone who does not love his brother, whom he has seen, cannot love God, whom he has not seen. And he has given us this command: Whoever loves God must also love his brother" (1 John 4:20–21).

This is a difficult lesson because sibling rivalry, to some extent, is apparent between all brothers and sisters. Nevertheless, a selfish spirit robs everyone of happiness, especially the one who carries it. You might discuss the older brother's reaction to his father's joy and how it interfered with this festive occasion.

The parable of the prodigal son contains at least four important lessons for life.

1. Mom and dad hope you learn to be wise early in life. Although you may not always agree with our parenting, most of our decisions will be based upon this premise.

2. When you dabble in misbehavior, ultimately you will face the consequences.

3. God and your earthly mother and father will always be there to forgive you when you ask for forgiveness with a truly repentant heart.

4. Real Christian love does not always seek its own, but rejoices with those who are happy and cries with those who are sad. Our love identifies us as Christians.

PERSONAL NOTES:

_____

_____

_____

_____

Week 1 Concept: HUMILITY

DEFINITION: Modesty; having a consciousness of one's own shortcomings; not proud or self-assertive.

USED IN CONTEXT: The football player showed great *humility* when he gave all the credit for the win to his teammates.

BIBLE VERSES:

"He has showed you, O man, what is good.
  And what does the Lord require of you?
To act justly and to love mercy
  and to walk humbly with your God."
  (Micah 6:8)

"Therefore, whoever humbles himself like this child is the greatest in the kingdom of heaven" (Matthew 18:4).

"God opposes the proud
  but gives grace to the humble."
  (James 4:6b)

DISCUSSION QUESTIONS:

1. Does being humble mean you shouldn't feel good about yourself?
2. Is there a distinction between feeling good about yourself and arrogance?
3. Since God created us in His own image, are we not wonderfully made? Yet who deserves the glory? (See James 1:17.)
4. In what situation could you demonstrate humility?

PARENT: Balance is the key!

PARENTS' AND CHILDREN'S COMMENTS:

_____

_____

_____

Week 2 Concept: *INTEGRITY*

DEFINITION: The quality or state of being of sound moral principle; honesty and sincerity.

USED IN CONTEXT: The father demonstrated *integrity* as he was filling out his income tax forms.

BIBLE VERSES:

> "The man of integrity walks securely,
>   but he who takes crooked paths will be
>   found out."
>   (Proverbs 10:9)

> "The righteous man leads a blameless life
>   (walks in integrity, KJV);
>   blessed are his children after him."
>   (Proverbs 20:7)

DISCUSSION QUESTIONS:

1. Do you know someone who demonstrates integrity?
2. How can you demonstrate integrity at school? At home? At work?
3. Being a person of integrity is not always easy or popular. Can you think of a case where it would be difficult to display integrity?

PARENT: Integrity is one of those qualities best taught by example.

_____
_____
_____
_____

Week 3 Concept: CONFESS

DEFINITION: To openly profess faith; to admit one's guilt or wrongdoing.

USED IN CONTEXT: The woman *confessed* that she had not paid for the jewelry.

BIBLE VERSES:

> "If we confess our sins, he is faithful and just and will forgive us our sins and purify us from all unrighteousness" (1 John 1:9).

> "If you confess with your mouth, 'Jesus is Lord,' and believe in your heart that God raised him from the dead, you will be saved" (Romans 10:9).

DISCUSSION QUESTIONS:

1. Have you ever confessed your faith?
2. Have you ever confessed your wrongdoings to your parents? To God?
3. If we confess our sins, does God forgive us? (See First John 1:9.)
4. Do your parents forgive you when you do wrong?

5. Have your parents ever asked you to forgive them for something?

PARENT: There are times when we make mistakes in dealing with our children. Nothing heals a relationship faster or more completely than confessing when you have erred, asking your children's forgiveness.

PARENTS' AND CHILDREN'S COMMENTS:

_____
_____
_____
_____

Week 4 Concept: SACRILEGIOUS

DEFINITION: Disrespectful of things held sacred; irreverent.

USED IN CONTEXT: The *sacrilegious* man was known to often curse and swear.

BIBLE VERSES:

"Do not swear falsely by my name and so profane the name of your God. I am the Lord" (Leviticus 19:12).

"You shall not misuse the name of the Lord your God, for the Lord will not hold anyone guiltless who misuses his name" (Exodus 20:7).

"You turn things upside down,

as if the potter were thought to be like the
   clay!
Shall what is formed say to him who formed
   it,
   'He did not make me'?
Can the pot say of the potter,
   'He knows nothing'?"
      (Isaiah 29:16)

DISCUSSION QUESTIONS:

1. Have you ever witnessed sacrilegious behavior?

2. How should we respond when someone
demonstrates irreverent behavior in our
presence?

3. Why is sacrilegious behavior so wrong?

PARENT: This is a good time to stress behavior
while in God's house. Children need to show
respect for church sanctuaries before, during
and after services. Do you allow your children
to run around, bang on the instruments or
fool around in the sanctuary while you are
visiting after church?

PARENTS' AND CHILDREN'S COMMENTS:

_____

_____

_____

_____

SEPTEMBER

Getting to Know You

Several years ago I spoke at a father-daughter campout in northeastern Ohio. Around the campfire one evening I shared some values and communication exercises. The purpose of this session was to provide dads and their daughters the opportunity and the means to relate with one another. It was a time to express feelings and values that do not ordinarily occur in everyday conversation.

I am convinced that each dad was attending this weekend experience because he cared for his daughter. Nonetheless, many loving parents either have difficulty communicating with their children or do not take the time to share with them in a meaningful way. I wonder if these men really understood their children's beliefs and values? Did the children understand their dads' beliefs and values? Had the parents purposefully and consciously taught their children those values they considered essential for life? These were the questions I had concerning the people in attendance that evening by the crackling campfire. Periodically I need to ask myself the same questions.

For an opening exercise that night we began by playing the "thumbs" game. Fathers and daughters paired up with one another as partners. Then in response to the following statements, they signaled their feelings by using their thumbs. You can enjoy this same exercise with your children. You might want to modify the statements to better accomplish your goal and suit the needs and ages of the participants. You may also want to designate items for just one person rather than both people responding simultaneously.

DIRECTIONS: In response to a statement you strongly agree with simply make a "thumbs up" sign. If you strongly disagree with the statement make the "thumbs down" sign. If you have mixed emotions about the statement give the "wishy-washy, uncertain" sign by rotating your open hand.

It is best to begin with easy and nonthreatening statements. In time you can work into more personal and meaningful material.

FUN ISSUES

1. Pizza is better than green beans.

2. Ice cream is better than pizza.

3. Gymnastics is my favorite sport.

4. The Cleveland Browns are my favorite football team.

5. I'd rather live on a farm than in the city.

6. I like the ocean better than the mountains.

7. Going to the library is more enjoyable than going to the zoo.

8. Swimming is more fun than bicycle riding.

9. Loud music gives me a headache.

10. Summer is my favorite season of the year.

RELATIONSHIP ISSUES

11. If you love someone, it's important to tell them.

12. If you love someone, it is easy to tell them.

13. Sometimes when I'm trying to talk to you, it seems like you aren't really listening.

14. I like it when you put your arms around me and hold me.

15. I'm not too big to hug.

16. Sometimes I feel like no one understands me.

17. Sometimes I feel confused about what you expect of me.

18. This little exercise is fun for me.

19. When I have a problem I feel comfortable talking about it with you.

20. I wish we could spend more time together.

21. I love you.

22. I've learned something about you today.

23. Sometimes you hurt my feelings and you don't even know it.

24. (Verbalize.) On a scale of 1 to 10—1 meaning yuk and 10 meaning great—I would rate our family:

25. (Verbalize.) Using the same scale I would rate my life in general:

26. (Verbalize.) Name one thing that would help raise the scale of #24 and #25.

MORAL AND SPIRITUAL ISSUES

27. If I saw somebody stealing I would ignore it.

28. We pray enough as a family.

29. I am confident that the Lord loves me.

30. Living the Christian life is easy for me.

31. Sometimes I get confused about things.

32. I have a bad habit that I'm trying to break.

33. Alcohol used in moderation is OK.

34. I enjoy going to church (Sunday school).

35. (Verbalize.) If Jesus were here right now, I would ask Him:

At any point in the exercise you may want to discuss a particular response. However, I would suggest that if you find your child's response somewhat disturbing you wait sometime before discussing it. Otherwise, your child may not feel entitled to be fully honest with you. We do not want to inhibit a child's response and have him or her simply say what he or she thinks we want to hear. We want our child to be honest with us. If we deal correctly with our responses, we gain a real understanding of the child's world as he or she sees it. Late that day or some other time we might say to our child: "Dana, I noticed when we played 'thumbs' the other day you said you felt like no one understands you. Could you tell me about that?"

Be sure you don't approach your child in an accusing or harsh manner. Otherwise he or she will clam up and the relationship will be hurt. If you feel it necessary to discuss the issue at the moment it occurs you might ask permission. "Would you like to tell me more about this?" In either case you are approaching the child in a respectful manner, one which will open the door for more meaningful discussions in the future.

COMPLETE THE STATEMENT GAME

Another interesting exercise involves finishing incomplete statements. This technique is helpful in working with children who have difficulty verbalizing their feelings. If a child is too young to read or write, the parent can read the statement and record the child's response. Not only can you gain insight into the child's thinking, but the child's recorded responses are precious memories. This particular form was taken from *Understanding and Treating the Difficult Child*, by Dr. Foster Cline.

Below are our three children's responses to this game, completed during a vacation trip in the spring of 1985. Carolyn was four, Hannah seven and Ben nine at the time. The italicized section is the statement you give the children—the remainder is our children's response.

CAROLYN 3/3/85

I'm afraid in the dark.
My greatest worry about God.
At home I clap my hands.
My family does pray to God.
I wish I could stop wetting my bed—but I did.
Mom and I do stuff—like play.
When I get mad I'm madder.
Most girls hold hands.
I hurt when I fall down.
I'm sad when you and Mom go away. I worry about you guys a little bit.
When I grow up I'll be a band lady—but I don't want anybody to watch.
I need someone's hand to hold when I go to bed.
Dad and I talk about good stuff.
I wish that I got a cat and a dog.

It would be funny if I rolled around in a sauna whirl tub.

I want to know if you would come home when I was at Nonny's.

HANNAH 3/29/85

I'm afraid of heights.
I know I can walk home from school.
I secretly whisper.
My greatest worry is parties.
Sometimes it's hard walking home by myself.
My mind tells me what is right and wrong.
At home I like friends to come over.
My mom won't give me a cookie.
My family loves me.
I wish I could stop my grandpa from smoking and my friend from kissing me.
Mom and I are friends.
When I get mad I scream.
Most girls play with Barbie dolls, but I don't.
When I was young I was cute.
I'm different because my name is spelled the same frontwards and backwards.
I hurt when I fall.
I'm sad when I have to leave my friends.
When I grow up I'm going to be a doctor.
I need love.
Dad and I love each other.
I wish I had lots of money.
I hate falling down—when I get hurt.

179

It would be funny if Dad sang in the shower.
Most boys have Go-bots.
I want to know if my mom's OK (she had an earache).
My school is fun.
Another wish I have is I would have magic. I could say "alakazam" and be home from school and not have to walk.

BEN 3/29/85

I'm afraid when I'm all alone.
I know I can do things with God.
Other kids play with me.
People often play with me and sometimes make fun of me.
My greatest worry is when I think God isn't with me.
My mind goes on lots of things.
At home I like helping out on things.
My mother won't get mad at me that much.
My family is very nice and sweet; I love them.
I wish I could stop being mean to Hannah.
Mom and I do lots of things together.
Most girls like me.
When I was very young I used to get spanked.
I'm different because I do different things than most people.
I hurt when people make fun of me.
I'm sad when someone dies that I like.
When I grow up I want to be a good basketball

player.

I need food to be healthy.

Dad and I do many, many, many, many, many things together.

It would be funny if Dad was a comedian.

Most boys/girls like to play with me.

I want to know what Dad and Mom were like when they were little.

My school is nice.

Three wishes I have are 1. knowing how God was there, 2. a new hand brake and 3. that everyone in the world loves God.

As a result of these exercises we have lots of good and humorous discussions. It is also good fun for the kids when mom and dad complete the sentences.

You can create your own lead-in statements to suit the needs of your family.

PERSONAL NOTES:

_____

_____

_____

_____

Week 1 Concept: AFFECTION

DEFINITION: A fond or tender feeling; a warm liking; devotion.

USED IN CONTEXT: The little girl was very *affectionate* with her mom and dad.

BIBLE VERSES:

> "We loved you so much (fond affection, KJV) that we were delighted to share with you not only the gospel of God but our lives as well, because you had become so dear to us" (1 Thessalonians 2:8).

> "God can testify how I long for all of you with the affection of Christ Jesus" (Philippians 1:8).

DISCUSSION QUESTIONS:

1. Who are the most affectionate people you know?
2. When and with whom is it good to share your affection?
3. What is an appropriate way to demonstrate affection?
4. If someone is being affectionate with you and you don't like it, is it OK to tell them?
5. What could you say or do if this happens?
6. Is there someone with whom you need to be more affectionate this week?
7. How does God show his love for you?
8. Did you ever consider that God can love others through you?
9. How do you like to express your affection?

PARENT: Children can benefit from your affection in one of three ways: overtly—a hug, a kiss, a pat on the back, a wink or a smile, a statement of love; covertly—three hand squeezes for "I love you"; vicariously—affection given to your spouse is a warm, secure feeling for the onlooking child.

PARENTS' AND CHILDREN'S COMMENTS:

_____
_____
_____
_____

Week 2 Concept: DISCIPLE

DEFINITION: A pupil or follower.

USED IN CONTEXT: His *disciples* believed him.

BIBLE VERSES:

"All men will know that you are my disciples if you love one another" (John 13:35).

"Therefore go and make disciples of all nations, baptizing them in the name of the Father and of the Son and of the Holy Spirit, and teaching them to obey everything I have commanded you. And surely I will be with you always, to the very end of the age" (Matthew 28:19–20).

NOTE: A disciple of Christ is one who believes what He has taught, accepts His sacrifice, receives His Spirit and lives by His example.

DISCUSSION QUESTIONS:

1. Are you a disciple of Jesus?

2. If so, in what ways can you demonstrate your discipleship?

3. If you aren't certain about your relationship with the Lord, study His words to you in Scripture. (Read the Gospel of John.)

PARENT: Your example is important. If your children do not see you actively being a disciple of Christ, don't expect them to be dedicated either. Areas like church attendance are important. Do you drop your kids off at Sunday school while you go have breakfast? Do they see you staying home from church when something good is on television?

PARENTS' AND CHILDREN'S COMMENTS:

_____

_____

_____

_____

Week 3 Concept: CONTRIBUTE

DEFINITION: To give or provide jointly with others; be partly responsible.

USED IN CONTEXT: The little girl *contributed* part of her allowance for the Sunday school offering.

BIBLE VERSES:

"Calling his disciples to him, Jesus said, 'I tell you the truth, this poor widow has put more into the treasury than all the others. They all gave (contributed, KJV) out of their wealth; but she, out of her poverty, has put in (contributed, KJV) everything—all she had to live on' " (Mark 12:43–44).

DISCUSSION QUESTIONS:

1. In what ways do you contribute your talents and energy to your family?

2. Are there other ways your parents would like you to contribute to the family?

3. The Bible tells us to contribute a portion of our money to the church. In what other ways can we contribute to the Lord's work?

PARENT: One of the greatest needs we have as humans is the feeling of belonging. Subsequently, we often feel this sense of belonging as we give of ourselves. Look for appropriate ways each of your children can feel he or she is contributing to his or her family and church.

PARENTS' AND CHILDREN'S COMMENTS:

_____

_____

_____

_____

185

Week 4 Concept: GENEROSITY

DEFINITION: Willingness to give or share; being unselfish.

USED IN CONTEXT: The fifth grader showed *generosity* by giving half of his allowance to the organization helping starving people in Africa.

BIBLE VERSES:

"Whatever you did for one of the least of these brothers of mine, you did for me" (Matthew 25:40b).

"Each man should give what he has decided in his heart to give, not reluctantly or under compulsion, for God loves a cheerful giver" (2 Corinthians 9:7).

"It is more blessed to give than to receive" (Acts 20:35b).

DISCUSSION QUESTIONS:

1. Could generosity pertain to things other than money? (time, encouragement, helping out)
2. How can we demonstrate generosity in our family?
3. In what ways can you improve in being a cheerful giver?
4. If we become generous, what does the Bible promise? (See Luke 6:38.)

PARENT: Two of the greatest gifts you can give your children are your time and your example.

PARENTS' AND CHILDREN'S COMMENTS:

_____

_____

_____

_____

OCTOBER

Faith

Boys and girls need to understand the importance of faith in the Christian life. Without faith it is impossible to please God (Hebrews 11:6). Ephesians 2:8–9 clearly indicates that faith is the means by which we have a saving relationship with God. Therefore, faith is not only important but essential to knowing and pleasing God.

But what is faith? Where does it come from? How do we get it? How does it increase? These are issues that need to be discussed with our children. Such spiritual concepts are rather abstract and difficult for youngsters to fully comprehend. Nevertheless, that is no reason to deprive children of early exposure to God's truths. Indeed, age is no barrier to relating personally with Him, and that begins with faith.

Faith means to believe or trust. For a concrete and practical approach to this topic try taking your child on a trust walk. To do this, blindfold your child and indicate that you will be his or her eyes for the next several minutes. You can lead your child by holding his or her hand and allowing the child to experience faith in your guidance.

During your trustwalk, take things very slowly in the beginning. Walk to a tree and let the child feel the rough bark or a weathered leaf. Give him or her the opportunity to smell a lilac bush or hear water rushing from a faucet. It is even more meaningful if you agree not to speak during your walk. Of course, you will want to be very alert to avoid a low-hanging branch, a hole in the ground or anything that might impede the child's progress or confidence in you. When approaching a curb or a step, stop and tap your foot to indicate a change in elevation. Eventually you both may feel comfortable enough to run together. When you are finished, your child may wish to reverse the roles and blindfold you. Now that's really putting faith to the test!

Some meaningful discussion can result from this trustwalk as you personalize the experience. In your conversation be sure to explain that God often guides us when things are not clear to us. He is worthy of our faith, and His Word is a "lamp to [our] feet and a light for [our] path" (Psalm 119:105).

To clarify this point a bit further, you can use

the following example. In 1927 a sculptor named Gutzon Borglum began his mountain carving in the Black Hills of South Dakota. Today Mt. Rushmore stands as a national monument of incredible dimensions. The presidents' heads are 60 feet high and each nose is 20 feet long. It is a beautiful sight when viewed from far off. But can you imagine looking over Borglum's shoulder as he carved out the mole on Lincoln's face? Unless the artist told you specifically what he was carving, there is no way you could determine what feature he was sculpting or how it fit into the scheme of things. It is only as you stand before the mountain that your perspective takes on significance and meaning.

Even so, God sees life and life's situations in unmatched and unfathomable clarity. What might be a blotch in stone from our perspective may be a portrait to God.

Furthermore, it is not merely the amount of faith that is essential. It is the object of our faith that makes the difference. If we have great faith in a wobbly chair, we're going to land on the floor. As Christians we can be certain that with God as the object of our faith we will ultimately land on our feet.

Where do we get faith? "Faith comes from hearing the message, and the message is heard through the word of Christ" (Romans 10:17).

In other words, faith results from either hearing God's Word spoken or reading it in the Scriptures. Consequently, the more time we spend with God in prayer and in reading His Word, the greater our faith.

In Luke 17 Jesus speaks about the issue of increasing our faith. He begins in verse six by inferring that faith can do the impossible. The things that appear to be out of the realm of possibility to people can be accomplished if we simply act upon the promises of God. Just as an exercised muscle grows bigger and stronger, so too does an active faith. God will bless our faith even if it begins the size of a mustard seed. Can you think of an area in your life where you can step out in faith and let God fully bless you? Not only will it increase your faith, but allowing your children to see you express your faith in God in this way will have a profound effect on them.

The analogy in verse seven regarding the slave in the field refers to the Christian life. The slave, bond servant or believer, in order to maximize his or her faith, must serve above and beyond the normal expectation.

Another principle that fosters growth in faith is found in verse eight. We exercise faith by serving God. Paul and Barnabas were ministering to the Lord when God called them out to begin the great missionary movement.

In the story about the 10 lepers being cleansed (verses 11–17) all were healed because of their faith, but only one turned back to thank and glorify God. What a sad commentary on truly loving the Lord—even after He had so richly blessed them. Perhaps we need to look at our own lives in this regard and consider our devotion to Him.

Finally, it is important to recognize the fact that all we have comes from God (1 Corinthians 4:7). Our faith abounds in humility. Our intelligence, energy, talents, compassion and "every good and perfect gift is from above" (James 1:17a). As we submit to God's leading through obedience and humility, faith will surely increase.

SUMMARY OF TEACHING POINTS ON FAITH:

1. Faith comes from God.
2. Faith is pleasing to God.
3. Faith means to trust.
4. God is worthy of our faith.
5. God will increase our faith as we pray, spend time in the Word, serve others, love the Lord and walk humbly in obedience to Him.

For another meaninful activity consider reading together the 11th chapter of Hebrews, which records the faithfulness of many Old Testament women and men. Perhaps you can each select your favorite "triumph of faith" and discuss those characters with whom you each most closely identify. Rereading the Old Testament accounts of each character would be helpful.

PERSONAL NOTES:

_____

_____

_____

_____

Week 1 Concept: SIN

DEFINITION: The breaking of religious law or a moral principle; the inward state of the soul as well as the outward conduct of life. The moral character of a person's actions is determined by the moral state of his or her heart. The inclination to self-centeredness as opposed to submission to God is sin.

USED IN CONTEXT: Jesus died for our *sins.*

BIBLE VERSES:

"If we claim to be without sin, we deceive oursleves and the truth is not in us" (1 John 1:8).

"For all have sinned and fall short of the glory of God" (Romans 3:23).

"We all, like sheep, have gone astray,

each of us has turned to his own way;
and the Lord has laid on him
the iniquity of us all."
(Isaiah 53:6)

DISCUSSION QUESTIONS:

1. Sin is something we need to recognize in ourselves. What does the Bible say about God recognizing our sin? (See Psalm 69:5.)

2. Although the penalty for sin is death, Jesus became sin and died in our place. What does the apostle Paul say about this? (See First Timothy 1:15.)

3. How can we get rid of the sin in our lives? (See First John 1:9.)

PARENT: The proper concept of sin, guilt and responsibility for our wrongdoing is very important to teach children. In our society it is popular to blame something other than ourselves for our own wrongdoing. Children who are taught to blame others for their own actions will not only have a tough time understanding their need for Christ as Savior, but as they get older they will have a hard time dealing with setbacks in life.

PARENTS' AND CHILDREN'S COMMENTS:

_____

_____

Week 2 Concept: REPENTANCE

DEFINITION: A feeling of sorrow for wrongdoing; remorse; consciousness of guilt; a change of heart.

USED IN CONTEXT: The man *repented* of his sins.

BIBLE VERSES:

> "God have mercy on me, a sinner" (Luke 18:13).

> "Repent, then, and turn to God, so that your sins may be wiped out, that times of refreshing may come from the Lord" (Acts 3:19).

> "If we confess our sins, he is faithful and just and will forgive us our sins and purify us from all unrighteousness" (1 John 1:9).

DISCUSSION QUESTIONS:

1. Why do you think God wants us to repent?
2. Do we ever get too old or too good for repentance?
3. Do you have some things you need to tell God about today?

PARENT: It is important to teach your children that when they do something that bothers you it is good for them to say they are sorry and mean it by not doing it again. Sin bothers God. But He tells us to repent, and He will always forgive us. (It is important to ask your children for forgiveness when you wrong them as well.)

PARENTS' AND CHILDREN'S COMMENTS:

_____

_____

_____

_____

Week 3 Concept: SALVATION

DEFINITION: Redemption; a saving or being saved; spiritual rescue from sin and death.

USED IN CONTEXT: Many churches today don't teach about *salvation*.

BIBLE VERSES:

"For God so loved the world that he gave his one and only Son, that whoever believes in him shall not perish but have eternal life" (John 3:16).

"I am not ashamed of the gospel, because it is the power of God for the salvation of everyone who believes" (Romans 1:16a).

"Salvation is found in no one else, for there is no other name under heaven given to men by which we must be saved" (Acts 4:22).

DISCUSSION QUESTIONS:

1. Why does the Bible teach that salvation is

necessary? (See Romans 3:23 and 6:23.)

2. What is God's provision for our salvation? (See Romans 5:8.)

3. How do we receive salvation? (See Romans 10:9 and Acts 16:31.)

PARENT: Salvation is an important decision. Have you experienced salvation? If yes, ask this question of each of your children. If you already know they have experienced salvation, have them explain what they did to receive it. Then praise the Lord together for saving all of you. Perhaps end your together time by praying for family members and friends who have not experienced salvation.

PARENTS' AND CHILDREN'S COMMENTS:

_____

_____

_____

_____

Week 4 Concept: REVERENCE

DEFINITION: A feeling or attitude of deep respect, love and awe, as for something sacred.

USED IN CONTEXT: The old man handled his tattered Bible with _reverence_ and care.

BIBLE VERSES:

"That at the name of Jesus every knee should bow" (Philippians 2:10a).

"Therefore, since we are receiving a kingdom that cannot be shaken, let us be thankful, and so worship God acceptably with reverence and awe" (Hebrews 12:28).

DISCUSSION QUESTIONS:

1. Who is worthy of our reverence? Why?
2. Have you ever seen people acting irreverantly?
3. List the various ways you can demonstrate reverence.

PARENT: Is God revered in your home? In what way? How do your children know that God is honored in your home? How would people entering your home know that God is honored?

PARENTS' AND CHILDREN'S COMMENTS:

_____

_____

_____

_____

NOVEMBER

Emotions

Wise behavior includes the appropriate expression of feelings. This is especially important because the average person experiences a wide range of feelings during the course of each day.

Feelings are common to people and reflect the very spice of our existence. Life without feelings is tantamount to mashed potatoes without gravy or butter. Without sorrow, joy has no meaning. The absence of pain obscures the blessings of comfort. If we've never experienced loneliness, neither can we appreciate fellowship. Feelings are a necessary part of life.

Nevertheless, children need to be taught correct ways to express their feelings. And, to a certain extent, they can choose how to feel. Children, especially moody ones, need to be lovingly confronted. Something such as: "Some children enjoy being happy and others enjoy being grumpy. Which describes you today? I can appreciate your being bummed out from time to time, but it makes better sense to work your way out of it."

Philippians 4:8 is the original text on the subject of the power of positive thinking. "Finally brothers, whatever is true, whatever is noble, whatever is right, whatever is pure, whatever is lovely, whatever is admirable—if anything is excellent or praiseworthy—think about such things."

I am certainly willing to empathize with a child who is feeling depressed or grumpy, but I in no way want to reinforce negative feelings. Furthermore, feeling poorly is no excuse for disregarding the feelings of others. On more than one occasion I have reminded our children to treat their brother and sisters with the same respect they receive from me, regardless of their momentary disposition.

But what about anger? Is anger a sin? Are we to repress anger or vent our feelings at any cost? The Bible says to be slow to anger and always settle it before you go to bed. It is a picture of balance. Repressed anger will often resurface in forms of guilt, depression and general unhappiness. However, indiscriminate expression of anger has its own set of problems. The fact is, children need to be taught appropriate and acceptable means of self-expression.

When Hannah was very young she had a difficult time verbalizing her angry feelings. She would bottle up emotionally until her little body literally shook. For a period of three or four weeks we had to methodically teach her how to verbalize and release her feelings when she became distressed. Of course, parental teaching is more readily learned when the parties involved are not in conflict. Therefore, at a time when things were running smoothly we began discussing the problem. Eventually Hannah practiced looking at me and verbalizing, "Daddy, it makes me mad when you do that!" We worked it through several times before she could actually apply it in the midst of conflict. This type of response is not only socially acceptable, but mentally healthy as well.

The source of a child's anger may vary from feelings of indignation (being teased or embarrassed) to selfishness or defiance (not wanting to go to bed). If I have unjustly wronged my child, I appreciate her telling me. If she is protesting a policy, I don't mind hearing her out, but it doesn't necessarily mean I will change my decision.

The following chart gives examples of acceptable and unacceptable expressions of anger. It is important for children to learn this and just as important for parents to not only teach it, but learn it themselves as well.

WHAT CAN I DO WITH MY ANGER?

Acceptable Behavior	*Unacceptable Behavior*
If it's not a big deal, ignore it.	Walk around with a chip on your shoulder.
If it bothers you and you need to deal with it, verbalize your feelings with that person face-to-face. Talk it out.	Name calling. Swearing. Hitting yourself or others. Throwing things.
If talking is not possible, write a letter.	Turn your anger inward.
Return kindness for evil. Love your enemies and pray for those who persecute you.	Get even.
Forgive and get on with life.	Keep the bitterness alive. Continue to think and stew about it.
These are not easy responses, but they are the best.	These often come naturally, but they are wrong.

A good activity is to find pictures that portray various emotional expressions. As you review these pictures, identify the emotion and discuss the different ways it can be expressed. It is also good to recall specific times when you have personally experienced such feelings.

PERSONAL NOTES:

_____

_____

_____

_____

Week 1 Concept: ANXIETY

DEFINITION: A state of being uneasy or apprehensive about what might happen; worry.

USED IN CONTEXT: The student is experiencing a great deal of *anxiety* thinking about the math test tomorrow.

BIBLE VERSES:

"Do not be anxious about anything, but in everything, by prayer and petition, with thanksgiving, present your requests to God" (Philippians 4:6).

"Therefore do not worry about tomorrow, for tomorrow will worry about itself" (Matthew 6:34a).

"Surely God is my salvation;
  I will trust and not be afraid."
    (Isaiah 12:2a)

203

DISCUSSION QUESTIONS:

1. Are there certain things that continually worry you?

2. What is the difference between being concerned about something and worrying about it?

3. What can you do to conquer anxiety?

PARENT: Remember the suitcase story mentioned on page 61? Be sure to give wise counsel to the child who is anxious about an adult area of concern. Perhaps the suitcase illustration will help.

PARENTS' AND CHILDREN'S COMMENTS:

_____

_____

_____

_____

Week 2 Concept: APATHY

DEFINITION: Lack of emotion; lack of interest; indifference.

USED IN CONTEXT: The entire class seemed *apathetic* during the social studies lesson.

BIBLE VERSE:

"So, because you are lukewarm—neither hot nor cold—I am about to spit you out of my mouth" (Revelation 3:16).

DISCUSSION QUESTIONS:

1. In what things do you have a great deal of interest?
2. In what things are you not at all interested?
3. Why do you suppose God finds apathy in our spiritual lives so distasteful?
4. Is there an area of your life in which you are becoming apathetic? If so, how can you work on it?
5. What is the opposite of apathy?

PARENT: Be sure to share with your children an area where you are apathetic but need to change. As they see you dealing with this problem, they will also desire to improve in a necessary area of their lives as well.

PARENTS' AND CHILDREN'S COMMENTS:

_____

_____

_____

_____

Week 3 Concept: TIMID

DEFINITION: Easily frightened; lacking self-confidence; shy.

USED IN CONTEXT: The *timid* little girl wouldn't raise her hand in class, even when she knew the answer.

BIBLE VERSES:

"For God did not give us a spirit of timidity, but a spirit of power, of love and of self-discipline" (2 Timothy 1:7).

"He said to his disciples, 'Why are you so afraid? Do you still have no faith?' " (Mark 4:40).

DISCUSSION QUESTIONS:

1. Although arrogance and boasting are not positive character traits, neither is timidity. Can you see how being timid could prevent you from being happy and getting things accomplished?

2. If you are somewhat timid, what are some things that might help you become more confident?

PARENT: If timidity is a problem for your child, you might help him or her set some goals to conquer it. Sometimes it is helpful for children to see this as a game of "child versus fear." The child wins the game by not allowing fear or shyness to keep him or her from doing the things he or she could do and should do. Promote the feeling that this child is a winner.

PARENTS' AND CHILDREN'S COMMENTS:

_____

_____

Week 4 Concept: CONTENT

DEFINITION: Happy enough with what you have or are.

USED IN CONTEXT: He was *content* with his new bicycle even though it wasn't brand new.

BIBLE VERSES:

"For I have learned to be content whatever the circumstances" (Philippians 4:11b).

"Then some soldiers asked him, 'And what should we do?' He replied, 'Don't extort money and don't accuse people falsely—be content with your pay' " (Luke 3:14).

DISCUSSION QUESTIONS:

1. Is it possible to be both ambitious and content? Explain.
2. Are you content with yourself at this time?
3. How do you think comparisons bring about discontentment?
4. If you are content, how does that affect those around you?

PARENT: The prayer of St. Francis of Assisi reads, "God, grant me the serenity to accept the things I cannot change, courage to change the things I can and the wisdom to know the difference."

PARENTS' AND CHILDREN'S COMMENTS:

_____

_____

_____

_____

DECEMBER

Saying No in the Face of Peer Pressure

Peer pressure is difficult to resist regardless of age. However, during adolescence peer pressure takes on added intensity. This is because the need for acceptance is at a premium, self-esteem is accosted daily and the ability to think abstractly has finally arrived.

Of course, putting into practice the various components in this book should add to the "immune system" of our children. In the face of peer pressure it is helpful for your children to have experienced the ways and means of saying no. One way to equip your children is by role playing. The following is an example that might be appropriate for your family.

Assume your daughter has encountered a dilemma in the backseat of a car full of kids drinking beer. Will she have the confidence to refuse, the self-esteem to resist and the sense to respond appropriately?

Set the scene: Four teenagers are driving around after a football game. You can set the scene by simply arranging chairs in the living room to simulate an automobile. If there are four people in your family make it a compact; five to seven people, make it a station wagon; over seven make it a van and write your own book!

There is no script per se, but the sequence of events might occur in this way:

Donna, the driver of the car, whips out a six-pack of beer and begins to guzzle. Shortly thereafter she offers a can to Shirley, the passenger seated next to her. Shirley declines, but after much persistence from the freewheeling driver, Shirley succumbs and begins drinking. Of course, Shirley and the driver expect everyone aboard to get loaded, so they turn their recruiting efforts to the backseat. Despite the urging, coaxing and even name-calling, the girls in the backseat remain steadfast and do not drink.

Betty, who is seated behind the driver, taps Donna on the shoulder and tells her to drop her off at the next restaurant. Betty leaves the car despite the jeering of her front seat companions and the silent stare of her former backseat companion, Barbie, and goes into the restaurant to call her dad for a ride home. The other girls continue on. If your chairs are old and resiliant, you might want to simulate a crash.

Proceed through the following questions:

1. Which girls in the group were strongest in character?
2. Which girl made the wisest decision?
3. How could this situation be avoided in the future?
4. Shirley, the first girl who was offered a beer, refused and then gave in. Why? Did she do what she thought was right or what someone else wanted her to do?
5. Barbie refused the beer and resisted the temptation to take it. Yet she left herself in a rather vulnerable position by staying in the car. What would you have done? Why?

For a scriptural application of this principle, read the account of Herod's birthday party, where he succumbs to peer pressure (Matthew 14). This story is also an example of when keeping your promise is a bad idea. Herod's pride prompted him to execute John the Baptist. Why? Because his dinner guests had witnessed a promise he had given to his stepdaughter. The entertainment that night became a dance of death because of pride and peer pressure.

_____
_____
_____
_____

Week 1 Concept: REPUTATION

DEFINITION: Estimation in which a person or thing is commonly held; character in the view of the public or the community; esteem.

USED IN CONTEXT: The teenager had a good *reputation* in his school.

BIBLE VERSES:

> "And Jesus grew in wisdom and stature, and in favor with God and men" (Luke 2:52).

> "A good name is more desirable than great riches;
>   to be esteemed is better than silver and gold."
>   (Proverbs 22:1)

DISCUSSION QUESTIONS:

1. How do you establish a reputation?
2. What kind of reputation are you building for yourself?
3. What kind of reputation would God be pleased to see in you?

PARENT: What a child thinks of him or herself

will determine his or her lifestyle and ultimately his or her reputation. Continue to acknowledge his or her strengths and be a source of encouragement for him or her.

PARENTS' AND CHILDREN'S COMMENTS:

_____
_____
_____
_____

Week 2 Concept: ALCOHOLISM

DEFINITION: A diseased condition caused by habitually drinking too much alcoholic liquor; alcoholic poisoning; addiction to alcoholic liquor.

USED IN CONTEXT: The teenager had difficulty admitting that she was an *alcoholic*.

BIBLE VERSES:

"Therefore do not be foolish, but understand what the Lord's will is. Do not get drunk on wine, which leads to debauchery. Instead, be filled with the Spirit" (Ephesians 5:17–18).

"Wine is a mocker and beer a brawler;
   whoever is led astray by them is not wise."
   (Proverbs 20:1)

NOTE: Television commercials glorify beer and wine. The people in the commercials appear healthy, happy and often humorous. They fail to tell you about the harmful effects of alcohol. According to the Alcoholism Services of Cleveland:

• One out of every eight people become alcoholics. If your parent has a drinking problem it increases to one in four.

• Alcoholism is the third leading cause of death in America, just behind heart disease and cancer.

• 55,000 people die every two years of alcoholism—more deaths than in Vietnam during a 10-year period.

• Drunk driving is responsible for over half of the deaths on our nation's highways.

So the next time you see a clever beer commercial, think about the destruction it can cause and think for yourself!

DISCUSSION QUESTIONS:

1. How do television commercials portray drinking?
2. What message are they trying to get across?
3. Why do people feel the need to drink?
4. Even though it is against the law, why do so many teenagers drink?

PARENT: Make a file of magazine and newspaper articles on the risks of drugs and drinking to share with your family at an appropriate time.

PARENTS' AND CHILDREN'S COMMENTS:

_____

_____

_____

_____

Week 3 Concept: NICOTINE

DEFINITION: A poisonous substance found in tobacco leaves, cigarettes, cigars, pipe tobacco and chewing tobacco.

USED IN CONTEXT: *Nicotine* is named for Jacques Nicot, a French ambassador to Lisbon, who introduced tobacco into France in 1560.

BIBLE VERSES:

"You were bought with a price. Therefore honor God with your body" (1 Corinthians 6:20).

"Don't you know that you yourselves are God's temple and that God's Spirit lives in you?" (1 Corinthians 3:16).

NOTE:

• Did you know that pregnant women who smoke risk certain forms of retardation in their babies?

• Cigarettes are one of the major risk factors in

cancer, emphysema, heart attacks and other diseases.

• It is also an expensive habit.

• Over 33,000,000 Americans have quit smoking!

DISCUSSION QUESTIONS:

1. Can you name one good reason to start smoking?
2. Why do so many teenagers begin smoking?
3. Will you be wise enough and strong enough to say no to smoking?

PARENT: Make a file of magazine and newspaper articles that reveal the risks of smoking to share with your family.

PARENTS' AND CHILDREN'S COMMENTS:

_____

_____

_____

_____

Week 4 Concept: CHAMELEON

DEFINITION: Any of various lizards that can change the color of their skin; a changeable or fickle person.

USED IN CONTEXT: The *chameleon* changed from green to brown as it jumped from the tree to the ground.

BIBLE VERSES:

"That man should not think he will receive anything from the Lord; he is a double-minded man, unstable in all he does" (James 1:7–8).

"Let us hold unswervingly to the hope we profess, for he who promised is faithful" (Hebrews 10:23).

DISCUSSION QUESTIONS:

1. Can you see how acting like a chameleon could be a problem?
2. Assuming the chameleon principle is true, what type of children should you seek to be around?
3. Teenagers especially are vulnerable to being chameleons when peer pressure is involved. It takes real strength to do what you know is right when others are urging you to do otherwise. Can you think of a time when you stood firmly against peer pressure? How did it make you feel?

PARENT: People often behave like chameleons. We often act like the people with whom we associate. Chameleons change their color while people change their behavior. If we are with wise people we act wisely; if we run with a foolish crowd chances are we will act foolishly. Children need to grasp the reality and the importance of this concept.

PARENTS' AND CHILDREN'S COMMENTS:

_____

_____

_____

_____

NOTES

1. James Dobson, *To Be a Woman*, transcript from a cassette program (Waco, TX: Word, Inc., 1982), p. 120.

2. John David Purdy, *Dads Are Special, Too* (Wheaton, IL: Tyndale House Publishers, Inc., 1985), pp. 95–96.

3. Charles R. Swindoll, *Growing Strong in the Seasons of Life* (Portland, OR: Multnomah Press, 1983), p. 287.

4. Donald Dinkmeyer and Gary McKay, *Systematic Training for Effective Parenting* (Circle Pines, MN: American Guidance Service, Inc., 1982), p. 58.

5. Burton White, *The First Three Years of Life* (New York: Avon Books, 1975), p. 50.

6. Corrie ten Boom, *The Hiding Place* (Washington Depot, CT: Chosen Books, 1971), p. 31.

BIBLIOGRAPHY

Baxter, Sidlow. *Explore the Book*. Grand Rapids, MI: Academic Books, Zondervan Publishing House, 1960.

Berrey, Lester V. ed. *A Treasury of Biblical Quotations*. Garden City, NY: Doubleday and Co., 1948.

Bryant, Alton. *Today's Dictionary of the Bible*. Minneapolis, MN: Bethany House Publishers, 1982.

Dinkmeyer, Donald and Gary McKay. *Systematic Training for Effective Parenting*. Circle Pines, MN: American Guidance Services, Inc., 1982.

Dobson, James. *To Be a Woman* (transcript from a cassette program). Waco, TX: Word, Inc., 1982.

Purdy, John David. *Dads Are Special, Too*. Wheaton, IL: Tyndale House Publishers, Inc., 1985.

Swindoll, Charles R. *Growing Strong in the Seasons of Life*. Portland, OR: Multnomah Press, 1983.

ten Boom, Corrie. *The Hiding Place*. Washington Depot, CT: Chosen Books, 1971.

White, Burton. *The First Three Years of Life*. New York: Avon Books, 1975.

For more copies of

Little People, Big Choices

contact your local Christian
bookstore or call
Christian Publications toll-free:
1-800-233-4443